FEEL GOOD ABOUT YOURSELF,
LOSE WEIGHT, and KEEP IT OFF
with VIVATION

Patricia Bacall

BENESSERRA PUBLISHING
LOS ANGELES, CALIFORNIA

Copyright © 2012 by Patricia Bacall

Loving Yourself Thin is a registered service mark of Bacall and Associates, Los Angeles, California

All rights reserved. No part of this book may be reproduced or transmitted in any form or by any means, electronic or mechanical, including photocopying, recording, or by any information storage and retrieval system, without permission in writing from the publisher.

Published by Benesserra Publishing, 1827 Barry Ave., Los Angeles, California 90025

Printed in the United States of America

Library of Congress Cataloging in Publication Data

Bacall, Patricia

Loving Yourself Thin: How to Achieve Your Ideal Body Without Dieting or Deprivation/ by Patricia Bacall

1. Self-Help   2. Diets   3. Weight Loss

00-192604

ISBN 978-0970629876

Contents

	Foreword	v
	Introduction	vii
1	Diets Don't Work: Give Up Dieting Forever	1
2	Food - Exciting and Dangerous?	11
3	Relearn How to Eat: "I CAN have it"	15
4	Your Shopping Excursion	31
5	What's That Feeling? Hunger and Emotions	37
6	Change Your Relationship to Food Forever - Eating Guidelines	43
7	Stop Being Down on Yourself - Learn Positive Self-Talk	53
8	When Fat's Where It's At	69
9	Getting Rid of Excess Emotional Baggage with Vivation	83
10	Totally Living for Today	95
11	Put It All Together for the Life You Want	101

FOREWORD

What this method is NOT

Change is not easy...there is no magic bullet for losing weight – no straight line from here to there. It takes courage to *want* to change, to read this book, and to make the commitment to yourself that you WILL change.

Any weight loss method entails healing, despite what you might hear; it is not simply mechanical, like a formula, because any method you employ to change your body requires not only thought and planning, but emotions, action, and commitment.

So if you're willing to do what it takes, willing to change, willing to make the decision that you're going to accept the challenge of change and do it, rather than make excuses, commiserate with your friends, exchange stories about how hard it is, etc., I can help you.

Among all the people I've ever worked with and helped, there runs a common thread: an inkling or similar small thought that, underlying all their body and weight issues, lies some emotioanl reason they overeat, eat when they are not hungry, or keep weight on despite their best efforts to lose it.

And so, what we do together is simply uncover and heal those underlying emotional causes of overeating, overweight and negative body image, so that the thin "you" can emerge. Having healed those issues, the way is clear to follow *any* healthy living action plan that appeals to you, based on your values.

Actually changing your body and your relationship to it requires just a few things:

You have to *eat*.

You have to *breathe*.

You have to *move*.

Above all, you have to *heal*.

All of these things require commitment, but before you can do any of them, you have to have self-esteem and know that you're worth the effort. Just thinking or talking about them is not enough, action will be required of you. And underlying all action must be the belief that you deserve to achieve your goals. Or at the very least, a believe that you are walking a path that will lead you to increased self-esteem.

Because it *is* a journey. Your destination may change over time – you might start out in one direction and discover six months or a year down the road that your values, and what is important to you, have shifted to another focus.

But you need to feel every step of the way that your path is a worthy one – one that adds courage and integrity to your self-image, and contributes to your self-worth and wealth as a human being.

So ultimately, that is why you might want to do this – not specifically to get skinny, because that is not always the goal of *Loving Yourself Thin* – but to fall in love with yourself as the unique and wonderful individual that you are, and to prove to yourself that you are powerful enough to effect change along this path we call Life.

PB

Sept. 13, 2011

INTRODUCTION

For most dieters, food is seen as the enemy...

Will you be shocked if I say, FOOD IS NOT THE PROBLEM? It's not! Food is healthful and delicious and is meant to be enjoyed. But do you eat food or do you use it? If you use food for any other reason than to fuel your body and satisfy hunger, then you are using food for things that it is not meant to solve. But still, food is not the problem, it's your inability to deal with life's stresses and your negative emotions. The goals of this book are several: to help you achieve the ability to feel comfortable around food, to be able to eat when you're hungry and stop when you're full; to teach you that you can enjoy the food you eat without guilt or self-recrimination, develop the motivation to create your ideal body, and enjoy increased happiness, satisfaction, well-being and creativity in all areas of your life.

The first and most important goal is to allow you to end dieting forever, because in the long run, diets don't work. You will be able to eat what you like, as long as you're following the eating guidelines, and lose weight. You will completely change your relationship to food and eating. You will learn to view food as something pleasurable that you eat when you are hungry to fuel your body. You will learn to avoid using food as an all-purpose solution for everything from loneliness to boredom. You will be able to eat anything that you love and enjoy, in the right amounts for you, without feeling guilty or ashamed. By learning how to feed yourself in ways that are self-loving and nurturing, you will stop eating more food than you need, lose weight, reach and maintain your ideal weight without dieting or deprivation.

When you begin to experience freedom from overeating and compulsive behavior, you will start to discover how much more creative energy you have to spend on constructive projects.

You will learn to admire and respect yourself for your own uniqueness and abilities and feel better about yourself, exactly the way you are right now. You will find that loving yourself as you are now assists in motivating you positively and paves the way for lasting changes.

Many dieters think that if they stop dieting their body will sabotage them and grow wildly out of control. As a result, they are fearful of food and eating, and feel that their body is an adversary. Instead of relating to your body as a part of you that needs to be controlled and restrained, you will learn to be in harmony with your body. You will learn to become your own best friend, cheerleader and self-support system.

DO YOU USE FOOD OR EAT IT?

You will start to find other ways to deal with the uncomfortable and troubling emotions that are often the cause of compulsive eating and bingeing. There are a variety of ways you can deal with emotions; suppressing your feelings with food or another substance is probably one of the least effective and most damaging ways of coping. By learning to be gentle with yourself and recognizing that your behavior is a protective mechanism, you can begin to expand your awareness of the problem and open the doorway to the solution.

Finally, you will learn about "Vivation"™, a powerful self-improvement method for resolving negativity and managing your emotions that will greatly improve your sense of well-being. This technique will be used as a tool, along with all the other tools you will be learning, to continually appreciate yourself more and improve your life.

So, congratulate yourself on your courage to deal conclusively with your body, food and weight preoccupation. Get ready to embark on a fascinating journey, which will change the way you relate to food and your body forever.

This process brings lasting changes. I wish that there were a magic formula I could give you that could promise the same fast, dramatic results that some diet plans do. The truth is that this program is magical enough, because of the deep inner changes that will result from your willingness to engage in the exercises and processes. Don't be in a rush to manifest the outward changes, because by doing that, you will be hooking yourself right back into the diet mentality of looking for the quick fix or magic bullet. As you change inwardly and start to heal your relationship to food, eating and your body, the outer manifestation will follow. Your changing thoughts and beliefs about yourself will start to show in different ways. People will begin to compliment you on your changing appearance even before you think there are any changes. Your self-esteem will increase, and you'll start seeing yourself in a different light.

It's a good idea to be open to a new kind of strategy toward change, since nagging yourself thin didn't work. Along with many others who are successfully Loving Themselves Thin, I think you'll be pleased with the results you can achieve. So let's get started....

Chapter One
Why Diets Don't Work: Giving Up Dieting Forever

The first step in finding freedom from dieting is to recognize that diets really don't work. The wisdom of not dieting will become obvious to you as we investigate this further. Most people consider dieting to be the only way to lose weight. But the odds are stacked against you, emotionally and physically.

Remember all the times that you've been on diets. Perhaps you were fortunate and lost weight. In most cases, however, the weight doesn't stay off. You probably think it was something you did that resulted in your failure to maintain that lower weight, but the fact is that the diet failed you. Once you go off the diet, you will probably gain back all the weight you've lost plus a few pounds. In fact, this happens to 95-98% of people who do lose weight on a diet, so you're not alone. Diets have never worked in the long run and they never will. Let's look at the dynamics of dieting, and how it affects you physically and emotionally.

Your body learns to function at the level of fewer calories, saving its fat stores

When you restrict caloric intake and try to persuade the body to burn its fat stores as fuel, you create an artificial environment of famine for yourself, and your body compensates by becoming more thrifty with every calorie. Your metabolism, (the rate at which you burn food for your body's activities) slows down. This means that while initially you may lose pounds and some fat, you are training your body to function on less food and fewer calories. Everything else remaining equal, if you ever start eating more calories, it will be stored as fat. Your body is being trained to burn fuel slower, saving

> SUCCESS AT DIETING ALLOWS THE DIETER TO AVOID THE DEEPER ISSUES THAT CONTRIBUTE TO THEIR NEGATIVE SELF-IMAGE.

the fat for survival. After going off the diet, you will gain fat faster than you did before you ever started dieting.

As discouraging is this seems to you, it makes perfect sense from the point of view of your body. Being quite sophisticated intellectually, you know that you are probably not going to starve. People who feel they need to diet are surrounded by plenty. However, your body has not evolved to the point where it can distinguish "diet" from "starvation." So, when you self-impose famine, in the form of a restrictive eating plan, your body hangs on to its fat stores, and you burn your muscle fuel stores for your energy needs. Losing lean muscle mass through dieting further decreases your ability to burn calories. Since your muscles burn calories even while you're resting, you gain weight more easily eating fewer calories. So dieting creates a vicious cycle of eating less, but gaining more easily from every morsel you do eat.

The "yo-yo" effect on your body

When you go off the diet and go back to eating a normal amount of food for your size and build, your body is relieved that the "famine" is over, and busily goes about storing even more fat for the next period of "starvation."

This is what has allowed our species to survive, much to the dismay of the repeat dieter, because it creates the "yo-yo" syndrome of weight loss and gain. The dieter finds it ever more difficult to lose weight as time goes by. Unless you find a way to increase the body's ability to burn fuel, through exercise and other means, the unfortunate result will usually be weight gain after going off a diet.

Compulsive Eating and Self-Loathing: A Vicious Downward Spiral

In addition to the metabolic havoc that restrictive eating creates, dieting will bring an additional dismal and dysfunctional element to your life: compulsive eating and bingeing. Dieting and compulsive overeating are two sides of the same coin, because dieting causes

compulsive behavior through restriction and denial. How?
Let's take a look:

The more restrictive a diet is, the greater the binge-type behavior you will indulge in, because without making other changes, you can't go on denying yourself food. If food serves a purpose for you other than satisfying hunger, you will not be able to restrict yourself indefinitely from something you need. Even if the diet is initially successful, and the dieter loses weight, a "diet mentality" is being created. This is the idea that all problems can be solved by restricting your food intake and losing a few pounds! By losing weight, you think of yourself as "good." But what is on the other side of that coin? In most people's minds it means that if you gain that weight back, you are "bad." How do you think this affects your self-esteem?

Also, success at dieting allows the dieter to avoid the deeper issues that contributed to their negative self-image in the first place. When you make the decision that "my body is somehow not right," weight loss brought about by dieting is really only a temporary bandage over feelings of low self-esteem, which will surface later in some form.

When you restrict your eating, as on a diet, there is a "rebound" effect, that is both physical and emotional. You can control your eating for a certain amount of time, and then a "demon hunger" seems to take over, and you eat as if you will never get enough.

So, the vicious cycle of restriction, denial, self-loathing, shame and hope starts. The person goes on a diet, loses control of their eating, gorges themselves with food, feels self-loathing and disgust, is ashamed, vows to do better, starts the restricted eating plan again, loses self-control, etc. The destructive cycle goes on and on, resulting in not the slender body that was the original intention of the diet, but a person who feels like an overweight failure, because they didn't have the "self-control" to make it work. The diet didn't solve anything and created many more problems. The unfortunate aspect of it all is the emotional, physical and psychological havoc created by an idea that doesn't really work in the first place.

When you make your body wrong for being the way it is, you feel self-loathing and make an attempt to change your body through restricted eating. There can be several possible results:

1) You are initially successful at losing your excess weight, but when you go off the diet you slowly but surely begin to gain it back. You feel disgusted with yourself.

2) You can't stay on the diet, continually find yourself eating the "forbidden foods," lose respect for yourself because of your "lack of will power," beat yourself up, and vow to get greater control of yourself. The more you try to control yourself, the more "out of control" you feel. This only serves to make you even more upset and miserable, thinking of yourself as a failure.

3) You are successful at restricting your intake of food and lose some weight. However, by not having food to use as a buffer against uncomfortable emotions, these feelings begin to surface. Subconscious fears start to come to the surface and cause you to make conclusions like, "What's so important about being thin anyway?" or "He/she only likes me for my body." You end up gaining back all the weight you've lost because you are sabotaged by your unresolved emotions.

What can you do? Give up dieting forever.

You have to give up the idea that the only way to create your ideal body is by restricting your eating or by eating what someone else says you should. You can achieve your ideal body through positive motivation to reach your goals and by being gentle, loving and nurturing with yourself. As you start to examine what you think is important in life, (your values), you will be making food choices and lifestyle changes based on positive things that you want for yourself, ideas that you think will improve your life. You want to love yourself and enjoy your life, right? Start thinking of creating the body you want based on those positive goals for yourself and giving yourself what you want, not only in the area of food or eating, but in the larger arena of your life. It is rare to achieve a positive outcome from a negative motivation; if that were possible, the most negative people would be the happiest, and it just doesn't work that way.

You are going to be examining issues that will truly change your life if you allow these ideas to impact you and put them into practice. You will begin to see the reasons that you use food, and how that has served a purpose in your life. You can change your thoughts and behavior with regard to food, eating and your body, which will bring about changes in your body as well. As you realize that you deserve to pursue and have all the things you want in your life, your focus on food and eating will change. Food will not be as important to you, because you will not be using it to try to solve issues that can't be solved with food.

Make the decision to learn about and heal your issues with food and eating. Consciously choose freedom from dieting and compulsive behavior.

When you stop dieting, you will realize that you like being the one in control of your life, and that includes what and when you eat. Your appetites and desires are valid and should not be subject to the opinion of anyone. You can enjoy being the one to decide how you will provide for your desires. You need to make the decision that you will never again punish yourself for the way you look by denying yourself food again. Acknowledge where you are at right now and take responsibility for your life and your body being the way that it is. Start to make changes based on accepting that reality. To use an old phrase, this is the first day of the rest of your life. You can start to make changes based on what you want for yourself, now and in the future, instead of being at the effect of the circumstances of your past. If you realize that you have been using food to avoid being sexual, for example, heal your fears about sexuality, instead of using food to avoid the issue. I will show you how, but you must be willing to do the work. If you're not ready to do that, just acknowledge that you're not ready, and gently remind yourself that when you are ready, you will begin. Being honest with yourself is a great help in uncovering and healing the reasons you use food to avoid your feelings.

The decision to stop dieting is a bold step in the right direction. This is the first step to eventually finding freedom from dieting and compulsive behavior.

A note about "Homeplay"

After every chapter, there will be exercises to do, which will prompt you to think about your relationship to food, your emotions and what contributes to your dissatisfaction with your body. It's okay if you choose to do these now, or skip over them and start these exercises after you've read all the chapters in this book. It's also okay for you never to do them, it's completely up to you. They are called "Homeplay." instead of homework, because I don't want you to relate to them as something that you HAVE to do, as you did in school. It's not bad not to do these exercises, just notice that you don't want to do them. There's nobody looking over your shoulder or grading you on these exercises, they are presented simply to give you further insights into yourself. Use them as tools for self-knowledge and to assist you in feeling stronger and better about yourself and your relationship to food and your body.

HOMEPLAY

1. Your Childhood

Write down all you can remember about your relationship with food in your earliest years, such as, "As a child, how did I act like around food, did I eat everything that was offered to me or was I finicky?"

Was there enough food...too much food? _____

Were one/both your parents always giving you food? _____

Did your grandparents provide different eating opportunities for you? _

What were mealtime traditions? _____

What was the atmosphere like? (Cheerful, disciplined, tense)_____

What were my favorite foods? _____

Find out all you can about your infancy and early childhood, with regard to food. Look at pictures of yourself as an infant, to about the age of 3 years. Talk to your parents or other family members, if they are available, and ask them questions such as:

Was I breast or bottle fed? _____

Were there any feeding problems? _____

Allergy to formulas or foods? _____

Did my mother have any problems with breast feeding? _____

Ask your mother what her relationship was like with your father, if possible, and vice versa. If your parent gets defensive or feel threatened, just tell them it's for a class on genealogy.

How do you think your parents' relationship affected you?_____

How was your early childhood, in general? Questions: What was I like? Was I happy, good, rebellious, willful, , lonely, stressed, etc. Were you punished often? Write down notes on what you find and jot down your feelings about what you have learned. _____

_____

_____

If no one is available, or no pictures can be located, you can still complete this assignment by finding a quiet place and relaxing, doing some deep breathing, and then allowing images of your childhood to arise in your mind. Expect to have some feelings arise along with this self questioning and let yourself feel any emotions that may be connected to this process.

2. Self-Inquiry

Write out short answers, including any thoughts, beliefs or feelings that come up in response, to the following statements;

How I feel about being overweight _____

_____

Some of the reasons I want to lose weight are_____

_____

_____

Why I think it is important for me to lose weight _____

_____

_____

What I've tried to do to lose weight _____

_____

Some of the things I think I should do to lose weight are: _____

_____

_____

If I were my perfect weight, I would be, or my life would be (write down any ideas that come up, not just your perfect weight)_____

3. Deep Breathing/Relaxation

Twice a day, for at least 5 minutes each time, practice deep breathing and relaxation. This is easy to do: sit down comfortably in a quiet spot. Focus on your incoming and outgoing breathing. Take a deep breath and as you exhale, concentrate on letting go of the muscles you can control, saying a word such as, "relax," or just "aaahhh." Let go of any thoughts that arise and continue breathing and saying your word as you exhale. You may choose to schedule a time for this exercise, or just stop at various times during the day to do it.

4. Self Assertiveness

This exercise is done to increase your assertiveness. Often overweight people or those with a negative self-image have difficulty setting boundaries regarding what they wish to do for other people. Sometimes this stems from a desire to be liked. Because of low self-esteem, they have difficulty putting their wants and needs before those of others, and this develops into resentments that can cause overeating.

Begin to acknowledge to yourself that sometimes you feel like saying "no." This could be when someone asks you to do something, or when you have do something you don't want to do. Say "no" silently to yourself when you realize that you're facing something that you don't want. This is to allow you to acknowledge your ability to say no, and to increase within you the idea that your desires and preferences are at least as important as those of others'.

This week, say "no" silently to yourself as often as you feel like it. This may also sound like "I don't want to" and "I won't." If you become aware there is something that needs to be done that you don't want to do, say that to yourself. Acknowledge that there's a conflict between what you want and what must be done. If it really needs to be done, you may want to do it anyway. The important thing is that you hear yourself say "No."

Acknowledge that, "No, I don't want to get up now," "I don't want to go to work," I don't want to do the dishes. " If traffic is a hassle, say, "I don't want to drive in this traffic, I don't want to hunt for parking," " I don't want to do what I am supposed to do," "I don't want to be a good girl and hide my feelings."

Say "No" to things you know you have to do, but have been putting off. Just tell yourself that you don't feel like doing them. Get honest, and you might find yourself doing them with pleasure.

Chapter Two
Food – Exciting and Dangerous?

Does any of the following strike a chord of recognition?

You feel like your life would be better if you lost a few pounds, and you decide to go on a diet.

You go on the latest diet and you restrict yourself from eating many of the foods you love. After a few days of restricted eating, you may notice that certain foods start to become more important to you, to seem larger than life in your imagination. Whatever your favorite foods may be, if you tell yourself you can't have them, they start to occupy a much greater than normal place in your awareness. In fact, you will probably find yourself obsessing about foods that aren't even your favorites. When you are on a diet, looking forward to lunch, you spend a great deal of your time that morning thinking about food, wishing that it was time to eat your lunch, obsessing about the candy bar you can't have, and generally being preoccupied with eating. Food becomes the "forbidden fruit," because anything that you or anyone else tells you that you can't have, you naturally want and crave. Tension arises because of your feeling conflicted abut eating. Much of your time and energy is used in this endless cycle of negative thinking that goes nowhere. This also detracts from your sense of well-being because by being on a diet, you're constantly reminding yourself that you're not okay the way you are.

You find yourself thinking about food and its effect on your body most of the time, whether it is beating yourself up for how you broke the "rules" during your last meal, thinking about how hungry you are, about what you "get" to eat at the next meal, about what you will look like if you are successful on your diet. You will probably notice yourself thinking of eating often during the day, because you are ignoring something about yourself that needs attention, and your day is filled with struggle, whether it is deciding to stay on the diet or denying that you are hungry. You flirt with the idea of how you can "cheat" on your diet and still get the results you want. Instead of being a means of enjoyably satisfying yourself and nourishing your body, food takes on a personality of its own and your own hunger threatens to sabotage you at every turn. Food becomes the "enemy," something to be feared and avoided. It can't be trusted, and you start to relate to food as if it can do bad things to you, without your consent.

Eating becomes dangerous, and you become obsessed with the idea that every time you go to nourish yourself, you are waging a battle. Who will win....your appetite or your will power? Even if you are victorious in controlling your appetite at this meal, there's always dinner with friends, a sumptuous buffet at a party, meeting someone for coffee, or that cute little donut shop down the street, beckoning to you to fill that void.

You can see how this takes up much of your time and energy that can be better spent in a variety of pursuits. This is not an enjoyable way to live, and yet dieters voluntarily experience these conflicts many times daily.

Does the scenario sound familiar? By going on a restricted eating plan and denying yourself the foods you love and crave, it sets up an obsessive relationship with those foods, which sets the stage for a lifetime of struggle regarding eating and your body. You create an intense longing for food that no amount of cottage cheese or carrot sticks can ever satisfy.

So food becomes both exciting and dangerous, the "forbidden fruit" that you flirt with and perhaps use to distract yourself from other issues in your life. You neglect developing yourself in other ways to become a full and fascinating human being because you think that if you are the "right" size, everything else will magically be okay. Food keeps you focused on your body as an object and keeps you from dealing with other issues in your life. You can talk endlessly with your friends about food, dieting, and exercise, but it doesn't help you solve your negative issues with your body. Dieting becomes an end in itself, where you feel successful if you lose weight, and despair if you don't.

Here's an exercise to do. Imagine that your body size and shape are frozen in time. There is nothing that you or anyone else can do to change their body. You can't work out to grow more muscle or burn fat, and there is no such thing as dieting to change your body size. You simply have the body you're given. Now finish the following statements:

If I could never change my body size or shape, I would _____

_____

_____

_____

What I would do differently is _____

_____

_____

Ways in which I would develop myself to create fulfillment and happiness _____

_____

_____

Never being able to change my body makes me feel _____

_____

Homeplay

1. Childhood Research

Continue your research by asking questions, finding pictures, etc.

In addition, find a child to observe, one of your own, a grandchild or relative. Spend an hour at a park or playground or other place where a number of small children are interacting with their parents.

Observe the little ones and notice how they relate to their parents, how they operate both dependently and independently, whether or not they have anything to eat, and if so, how they deal with food and how their parents deal with them.

Try to imagine what you were like at that age and how your interactions with your parents and with food might have been.

2. Deep Breathing/Progressive Muscle Relaxation

Twice a day, for 5 minutes each time, practice deep breathing, while mentally going through your body and suggesting to your various body parts that they can relax. Even if you feel awkward doing this, do the best you can. Notice if any parts of your body seem especially resistant to relaxation or dense with tension or feeling. You may choose to schedule a time for this exercise, or stop at particularly stressful moments during the day to do it.

3. Assertiveness

You are learning to say "no" in a positive and healthy way. Tell a friend or family member that you are learning about asserting yourself and ask them if they will be willing to participate in an experiment. If they agree, ask them if it would be all right with them for you to say "no" this week to something they ask you for, and that you will then discuss with them whether or not you are willing to do it anyway. Even though you might not really care about doing the thing, practice your ability to say "no."

Chapter Three
Relearning How to Eat

You eat for all kinds of reasons other than hunger, and it may be interesting for you to realize that this has served you in many ways. You eat to be social: since the dawn of time, mealtimes are also family gathering times. You eat when you're in pain, to soothe or sedate yourself. You eat to celebrate events, and you eat to reward yourself. Can you remember if you've ever used food as a reward for putting in a long day's work? So, food nurtures you in ways that are very primal, and even people who aren't compulsive overeaters sometimes eat when they're not hungry, for a variety of reasons. If you've gotten overly hungry, you might overeat. Or you may try to boost your energy when you're tired or bored. However, it's not healthy when you use food to avoid looking honestly at yourself, or to avoid certain feelings, and if you start to become aware of the ways that you might be using food, that is a good realization. You may notice that you eat to avoid feeling emotional pain. If you know that the way you eat is not helping you to feel good about yourself, start looking at the ways in which you use food to change the feelings that you label "hunger."

Many compulsive eaters never allow themselves to feel real hunger. They just eat all the time. They eat by the clock, thinking "It's noon...I must be hungry for lunch," instead of waiting for their body to signal them that they have used up the fuel from the previous meal and it's time for more. Sometimes people eat like preventative maintenance, they eat because they think they might be hungry later. Eating when you're not really hungry is to your body like trying to top off your gas tank when you don't need gas. In your car the excess fuel would spill out, but in your body the excess fuel gets stored as fat.

Some people feel guilty if they don't want to eat food that is being offered, so they eat it anyway, hungry or not. In certain cultures, it's completely normal to eat when you're not hungry, as in "What? You have to be hungry to eat? Since when?" Many people eat when they want to "be good to" or treat themselves. If you feel sad, lonely, or want to avoid feelings of boredom, food can be a comforting friend. Food can act as a sedative and soothe you when you're feeling angry or upset. Bingeing and its aftermath of self-hatred can effectively distract you and keep you from dealing in an effective way with a situation in which you're undecided about what to do. But food doesn't really solve any of these feelings or mind states, it just temporarily changes your experience. Eating or bingeing buffers you from the pain or intensity of your feelings. If you think about it, you can probably think of a few times that you've eaten when you weren't hungry, as we all have.

To help you clarify these ideas, finish the following statements:

Sometimes I eat when I'm feeling a little _____

_____

I feel especially hungry when _____

_____

I get a little anxious when _____

   It's especially important to be gentle with yourself about this, because the reason you use food is that you don't know what else to do with the uncomfortable feelings. You could use something a lot more destructive, like alcohol or drugs. So until now, food has been one of the best tools you've had to deal with unresolved emotions, and that's why you "use" food for a variety of reasons other than hunger. As you go along in the book, you'll be learning tools to help you cope better with your emotions, so you can use food for what it is meant to do, nourish your body.

Is this feeling really hunger...or what?

Sometimes you feel something in your body that you assume is "hunger," because in the past, food has helped to relieve it. But is it really hunger? Is it really your body requesting fuel for its functioning? Are you really, truly "hungry" all the time, as you may think you are? If you are a compulsive overeater or use food to avoid feeling emotions, you probably call many feelings "hunger" that are actually something else, like boredom, sadness, awkwardness or feelings of inadequacy. Since you have habitually used food to make these feelings go away, it is natural to relate to them as "hunger." Without blaming yourself, or making yourself wrong, can you recall a time when you ate when you weren't really hungry because it relieved tension of some sort?

Briefly write about it: _____

_____

_____

_____

"Being with" your feelings

How do you begin to get in touch of the entire range of emotions that can exist at times when you think you're feeling hunger? You can begin by recognizing that emotions can cause the desire to eat, masquerading as hunger. Start to pay attention to your internal cues. This means that you will start to really focus on the feelings in your body to determine if what you are feeling is hunger or some other feeling that can't be "fixed" by food. In order to do this, let yourself feel the feelings in your body that you normally would feed in order to make the feelings go away. Instead of going immediately for the food, pause and ask yourself,

Am I feeling real hunger or is this something else?

Do I need to tell someone something?

Am I upset about something?

Do I need to call a friend for some support and encouragement?

Am I feeling angry?

Do I want to cry?

Do I want a hot bath or a hug?

Do I feel deserving of a reward?

Am I eating to please someone else?

You won't always be able to tell exactly what is going on with you at the moment, but try to begin to discriminate between the feelings, just for a couple of minutes, the next time you feel like eating. You may be surprised at how quickly you start being able to distinguish between feelings of boredom, anger, sadness, and real "stomach-being-empty" hunger. As you start to get in touch with your natural sensations of hunger, you will find that you won't need to eat every time you feel something in your body. You will begin to recognize that certain feelings can't be healed by food, food only covers them up temporarily . The feelings will still be there, so using food is really only a momentary distraction. Give yourself some time and space to find the feeling that is asking for attention and "be with" that feeling by doing some deep breathing and relaxation while you're feeling it.

I can't tell you how many times I've had the urge to eat candy when I'm feeling frustrated or unmotivated to do my work. I now know that the feeling of wanting candy are emotions masquerading as "hunger." Instead of immediately going for the "quick food fix," spend some time with yourself exploring the urge. Look for a way to soothe yourself by giving yourself compassion and permission to have that feeling. Tell yourself that you understand and accept yourself, even if that understanding and acceptance aren't perfect. There's probably a good reason you feel as you do. Be on your own side. Notice that you would probably have compassion for someone else if they came and told you about it, so have compassion for yourself.

Feelings are constantly flowing

Stop being down on yourself for having a feeling, and the feeling with which you're struggling will begin to loosen its grip on you. By learning to "be with" them, you will soon start to notice that the feelings are patterns of energy that can flow through you without your needing to do anything to make them go away.

Some other statements that you might say to yourself are:

I'm open to this feeling teaching me something about myself.

The feeling I'm having is very human, I guess I'm pretty normal.

I'm really glad this feeling isn't worse.

I can relax even with this feeling.

Isn't it amusing that this feeling usually causes me to want to eat?

What a curious experience it is to notice that this feeling makes me want to eat.

Some statements that might be particularly effective for me when I'm feeling like I want to eat, but I know I'm not hungry are: _____

_____

Legalizing food and eating what you want

As a dieter, for as long as you can remember, certain foods are supposed to be off-limits to you. Indeed, you've probably permanently excluded whole food groups, including fats and sugars. However, have any of the "forbidden foods" somehow found their way into your mouth? So you may notice that, even with the best of intentions to abstain, the something in you which craves those foods demands to be fed. By telling yourself that you can't have it, you practically guarantee that you will eat it. Crazy, but that's the truth with many dieters.

Legalizing food will change all of that by allowing you to get out of the way of your own desires. What does that mean? If you want to deal with a charging bull, does it make sense to stand squarely in front of it and demand that it stop? Or to step aside and, like a skillful matador, allow it to thunder past? You may be covered with dust, but you're still standing. Legalizing food is like being a skillful matador with your food cravings…you allow them to exist, and respect them, and eventually they won't knock you for a loop.

A dramatic change

Legalizing food means that it's okay to eat anything you want, as long as it's exactly what you want and you are hungry. All food is legal for you to eat and therefore good. There are no bad foods. Telling yourself, "This is really bad for me, I shouldn't be eating this," while you are eating something is worse for you than any food could ever be.

This is definitely not a prescription to stuff yourself, and legalizing food doesn't mean that you gorge yourself on everything in sight. It simply means that you start changing your thinking that it is all right for you to eat any food. For most chronic dieters, this is like being let out of prison. It gives them a heady sense of freedom that is not without some fear. Most dieters don't trust themselves and feel out of control around food. But just the idea that you can eat what you want suggests that you can have the fundamental satisfaction of feeling fed, which opens the door to healing your chronic feelings of deprivation. (By the way, if this concept is not "you", or you don't relate to it, there's some other issue that will. Just keep reading.)

> I KNOW I CAN HAVE IT, BUT DO I REALLY WANT TO FEEL THE WAY I KNOW THAT I WILL FEEL EATING THAT PINT OF ICE CREAM?

This is such an outrageous concept, I'll explain it further. In learning to Love Yourself Thin, you will start to eat what you want and crave. What does this mean? It means that you will give yourself what you want, when you want it. It means that if you want chocolate cake, eat chocolate cake. Not the light, diet variety. Eat the richest, most delicious piece of chocolate cake you can find, as long as it will satisfy your desire. Legalizing food means that you will give yourself the food that you are craving, no matter how odd it seems. Some part of you wants it, so you should make the effort to go out of your way to give yourself the food that you love, whenever you want it. Even if it's mashed potatoes and gravy at 2:00 AM or carrot cake for dinner, that's what you should be eating. This means that even the foods that were your worst enemies when you were dieting, cookie dough and ice cream or whatever, are now legal for you to eat, whenever you want and (for now) in any amount.

By removing all artificial restrictions, you will have no need to rebel against any rules, even those you've set for yourself. You're stepping out of the path of the raging bull, and you can begin to make food choices based on what you want for yourself. You will find that by telling yourself it's okay to have chocolate chip cookies, you will eat three instead of a dozen, and not feel bad about it. When you can allow it to be okay to have eaten three cookies, you don't create feelings of guilt and self-recrimination about yourself. All of that negative energy is freed up for you to go about living your life more creatively and effectively.

That's outrageous! How can this approach possibly work?

You've seen that restricting your intake hasn't gotten you to where you want to be, and denying yourself the foods that you love has made you crave them even more, to the point of bingeing and hating yourself for it. Understandably, many people will have many fears about eating whatever they crave. They'll say, "If I just eat whatever I want, I'll never stop!" This fear is quite natural, and it's okay to allow yourself to have this fear, after all the years of programming and guilt.

But don't let your fear stop you from healing your food addiction with this new approach. Of course it is confronting all of your worst fears about your eating and your body. But has trying to restrict yourself from ever eating the forbidden foods really worked? By learning to not stand squarely in the path of your food cravings and getting knocked for a loop by them, you lay the foundation for freedom from compulsive behavior regarding your eating habits. You begin to say "yes" to yourself, and that part of you that has been insistent on eating the forbidden foods, no matter what, even though you promised yourself you wouldn't, will begin to get quieter. You begin to realize that you CAN have what you want, and it starts to become your choice about whether you will eat it.

"I can have it...but do I really want it?"

Give yourself the time to make the transition into allowing yourself to eat any and all foods. The truth about this is that you really can eat only so much cookie dough or candy bars before making yourself sick. Eventually your body says "Okay, I've had enough chocolate cake, I don't want any more right now." You begin to realize that you can have chocolate cake whenever you want it, and you don't crave it as much. As healing of your compulsive eating occurs, based on your values for yourself and what you consider to be healthy foods, you will begin to make the "right" food choices. You will be able to say, "Of course, I know I can have it, is it really what I feel like eating?" But only after allowing yourself to go through a period of "outrageous" eating, which is actually healing you addiction, can you get past your denial of giving yourself the foods you want and crave. This is the way to freedom regarding food and eating. A completely different approach is needed, and for many, this has been the way out of compulsive behavior and self-abuse. It reduces your fear and anxiety about food, and when you're less anxious, you will eat less.

No food is "off limits"

The amazing part is that as you go through all of your formerly "forbidden" foods in this way, eventually you start to realize that you can have them whenever you desire, and then you don't crave them as much. The part of you that has been deprived of satisfaction from eating begins to learn that it will no longer be deprived of the foods you love, it relaxes and eventually you will be satisfied eating appropriate amounts of your favorite foods. You will have the satisfaction of eating and feeling fed by exactly the foods that you love the most. This lessens your compulsiveness and anxiety about eating, because there is no reason to be compulsive about the foods that you know you can have. Allow yourself some time for this to occur, and be patient and loving with yourself as it is happening.

Watch what your mind does with this concept and be aware of the way you think about this way of feeding yourself. You must be aware that it's not a recommendation for eating everything in sight, and you must learn and follow the Eating Guidelines. Your goal is not to mindlessly allow yourself to be a glutton. Loving Yourself Thin is about increasing your awareness about your relationship to food and eating. You are in the process of becoming a connoisseur. It's the beginning of relating to food in a completely new way. The idea is to be able to tell yourself, "I know I can have it, do I really want it, or is it because I thought I couldn't have it that I want it?"

> IF YOU'RE FEELING THAT FAMILIAR FEELING THAT YOU USUALLY FEED, CHECK IN WITH YOUR STOMACH TO SEE IF IT'S REALLY HUNGER.

This is a process of nurturing yourself, so be patient, and expect thoughts like "I shouldn't be doing this," or "This is bad for me," to arise, and just take a moment to stop and appreciate what you are doing for yourself. Remind yourself that you are trying something different, because what you did in the past doesn't work for you.

EXERCISE:

Some of the things you might say to yourself are:

This is what my body wants, I'm taking care of myself.

I'm being good to myself, I'm nurturing and nourishing myself.

I'm taking care of what the child in me wants and craves, and through this process of feeding myself what I want, I am healing myself.

Whenever you hear yourself say, "This really isn't okay," that's the motivation to counter it with the positive message of "I'm trying a new approach to loving and taking care of myself."

As time goes on, and you continue to feed yourself what you desire, it will seem more and more natural for you to eat what you want and not give yourself any negative messages. You will simply pay attention to what you want to eat, and give yourself that. Ask yourself "What is it I really want to eat in this moment?" instead of just putting anything in your body. There will be times when you feel as if you're starving and you'll want to eat whatever is easiest, but more and more, you can develop an awareness of feeding yourself exactly the right food for your own satisfaction.

By feeding yourself with the foods that you really love, you are giving yourself the message that it is okay to have your desires, that you're okay the way you are. This allows your self-esteem to rise, and gives you the positive motivation to reach your goal of having your ideal body.

Also, you will be aware of how your food choices affect you with regard to your goals for yourself. When you know you can have a certain food, you have the choice to decide if eating it helps you move toward your goals for your body. Sometimes people see that it is not as important as they thought it would be to reach their goal of a perfect body in order to have an enjoyable lifestyle. As they calm down about their relationship to food and feel better about themselves as they are, they just naturally enjoy their lives more.

The choice is always yours, whether you want to experience the food in your mouth or the satisfaction of doing the things you have decided on for yourself, such as eating in a certain way. The important thing is that YOU approve of your choice and support yourself in making it. You may tell yourself, "I've decided to have this dessert, so I might as well enjoy it thoroughly, rather than making myself wrong for it."

In the homeplay section, write what foods you eat and when, and how you felt when you were eating it, especially if it is a formerly forbidden food (FFF). Also note why you think you chose that particular food, and see if that relates to anything in your past.

One of the major benefits that comes from this idea of eating what you want, when you want it, is having a lot less anxiety about food. If you feel that you are taking care of yourself, you will experience less stress. Thus, as you relax about the idea of controlling yourself, you will actually eat less.

> SOMEONE WHO HAS UNRESOLVED FEELINGS OF GUILT REGARDING SEX MAY AVOID BEING THEIR IDEAL WEIGHT BECAUSE THEY WANT TO AVOID ENTIRELY THE ISSUE OF SEX.

HOMEPLAY

1. Examining Your Ideas and Beliefs About Food

What messages have you received about food from your family? From society?

What are the messages you received as a child about food?

Were you told you needed to clean you plate before you could leave the table or before you could have dessert?

Were you told there are starving children in India, so you must eat all of your dinner?

As a child, how did these messages affect you?

My family messages were (or are): _____

_____

_____

_____

What were the phrases or things you were told about food growing up? _____

_____

Were you very poor or given the feeling that somehow there is never going to be enough food?

How are these messages still affecting you as an adult? For example, do you notice that you feel compelled to eat everything on your plate in a restaurant because it would be a waste of money if you didn't? Or that you must eat everything offered you when you are a guest for dinner because to do otherwise would be rude and insulting to your host? To explore this further, finish the following statement:

Sometimes I eat even when I'm not hungry because: _____

_____

Do you find that you stuff your feelings down with food because it's not OK to be angry? Or do you eat to soothe yourself when you're feeling particularly anxious?

Pay attention and be aware if and when you overeat and ask yourself if there is an early childhood message playing in your head.

3. "Being with" your feelings

When you notice that you are having an uncomfortable feeling that makes you feel anxious or upset, try to just "be with" with that feeling a little bit longer than you normally would before doing whatever it is that you do to deal with those feelings. For example: if you feel anxious or stressed out and you normally would make a trip to the vending machine to get a snack, let yourself "be with" the feeling of wanting that snack, and wait for a few moments before you go get it. Take a few deep breaths, relax as much as you can, and let yourself feel the feeling. See if you can notice if the feeling changes in any way while you're paying attention to it. Don't restrict yourself from having the snack, just delay it for a few moments while you inwardly explore your desire.

What happened when I tried this technique: _____

_____

_____

4. Assertiveness

Learning to say "no" in a positive and healthy way to other people. Notice how you feel about each request someone makes of you. If it is something that you strongly do not want to do, refuse to do it. Then negotiate with the person who made the request, so that either the task gets done some other way (if necessary), or both of you are satisfied even if the task does not get done.

For example, someone in your household asks you to run an errand for them and you don't want to because you are tired and want to stay home. Say, "No, I will not do it. I am tired now and want to rest." Then find out if there is any reason they cannot do it themselves. If they cannot, find out if it can be done later and who can do it. If it needs to be done right away, find out how the person can arrange to be satisfied even if you don't do it. Remember, there is often more than one solution to any situation.

How I used this technique this week and what happened: _____

_____

6. Food

Allow yourself to eat what you want, as much as you want, whenever you want. Make sure you are not stopping because you think you should or because you're afraid you'll gain weight, stop only when you feel satisfied. Pay attention - if you get to a point where you think you've had enough, relax for a moment and assess your level of satisfaction. Then if you still want to eat some more, go ahead. The important thing is for you to make sure you don't accidentally deprive yourself.

Some of my formerly forbidden foods that I ate this week were: _____

_____

_____

How I felt eating my FFFs (formerly forbidden foods): _____

_____

_____

7. This week:

Eat when you are hungry.

Eat exactly what you want to eat.

Eat until you are satisfied.

Don't stuff yourself mindlessly, eat with awareness of how the food tastes and feels in your mouth and in your stomach.

If you find yourself overeating, see if you can notice why you overeat. What messages do you give yourself when you overeat? What happened during the day on which you overate?

Try to be more gentle and compassionate with yourself than you have been in the past.

I overate on (fill in day) _____ because_____

_____

8. Compassion and understanding this week:

❑ None, I felt upset with myself

❑ A little, I could understand my behavior

❑ It was okay with me, I felt compassionate towards myself

❑ A lot, I felt I nurtured myself and my desires

Chapter Four
Your Shopping Excursion

One of the most interesting and profound exercises for you to do with your new way of feeding yourself is to write out a shopping list. This means you start to think about and write down all of your favorite and/or formerly forbidden foods. This list will probably be unlike any other shopping list you've ever written. Why? Because you will be reaching way back into your past, and considering any and all of the foods or snacks that you've ever loved or wanted to consider putting them on your list. It doesn't even matter if they're currently available, you may not be able to find some items, but the idea is that you can have anything that you want, so put it down on your list. No food is off-limits to you. This is a process of allowing yourself the freedom to create the mindset: "I CAN have it, do I really want it?" instead of your usual idea of "I can't have it."

Remembering that this is a learning and healing process for you, take your list to the market, go into all the supermarket aisles that you used to avoid, and purchase as many of the items on your list as you want.

You should expect to feel some anxiety about confronting all of the old taboos about what foods you should eat. You'll hear yourself saying things like, "This can't possibly work. What am I doing?" Also, fears about what people are thinking will come up, but don't let these ideas or fears stop you from going through with this process. Consider this an awareness-expanding field trip. Nurture yourself with thoughts of "I'm being good to my body and feeding it what it wants," and "This is how I'm healing my addiction to food." Be sure you bring home plenty of your favorite foods, because you don't want to run out. You should fill your cupboards with all the foods that you've always longed for, but rarely dared to buy or take home. Bring home much more of the formerly forbidden foods that you can possibly eat. Your thought, when surrounded by all of your favorites foods, won't be, "Should I eat it?" but, "Which of my favorite foods will I eat?"

This is a very powerful process and will give you amazing insights into your relationship to food, eating and your body.

This is about making peace with food and learning to live with your desires, not denying them and trying to make them go away as you've done in the past. The feeling and idea that you want to create is that you know you can have whatever you want, and that it's going to be available for you whenever you want. Over time, as you experience your ability to satisfy yourself with the foods you really crave, your body will naturally ask for a wide variety of foods. It may be cake or it may be salad, and it makes no difference, you simply give your body what it is asking for, and you leave behind forever the feeling of deprivation.

You will be amazed that, by legalizing foods, and consciously developing the mindset of "I can have it," that much of the charge of eating the food will be removed. You'll either eat it and say, "Gee, this is what I've been craving and denying myself all these years? I don't even like it that much!," or you'll say, "AAAHHH!," and a part of you will be deeply satisfied regarding that particular food. Either way, you will learn something about your relationship to that food, and will have lessened your compulsive relationship to food in general. When you legalize all food, it allows you to either have it or not. Part of the reason that you stuff yourself on a binge is that you think you are not supposed to have it, you can never have it again, and that this food will not ever be available to you. When you are feeding yourself your desired foods on demand, there will come a point when your body will say, "Okay this is enough." You will learn that your formerly forbidden foods will never be disallowed again. Your eating habits will begin to change. You will know that if you want a certain food, it will always be available to you, and this knowledge will lessen your compulsiveness.

After some time goes by and you allow yourself to have any food you want, you will begin to find that you are in a place where you can choose to eat it or choose to not eat it. When you get to the point of knowing you can have anything, you start to honor yourself with your food choices. When you can say "I can have that," the next question becomes "Do I really want that? How will I feel eating it and how will my body respond to that?" Think about the feeling that you'll have after eating it and make your choice accordingly.

Many people ask me, "I love and crave chocolate, but I have an allergic reaction to it, what should I do?" The answer is, be aware that you'll have a reaction to it and decide whether you want to experience that reaction. Take control by recognizing that it is your choice, don't give control to the food. You will either say, "I don't care, I want the chocolate anyway," or "Oh yeah, I remember feeling spaced out for an hour last time I ate chocolate, I don't want to feel that today, maybe I'll pass." You make choices based on what you like to experience more, the good taste of chocolate in your mouth or feeling good by not having an allergic reaction. If you decide to eat the chocolate and have a reaction, be gentle with yourself and say, "Well, today I felt like the chocolate. Maybe next time, I'll choose differently." Don't make yourself wrong for eating the chocolate, just notice that you're not ready to let go of it, and know that you will when you are ready. You see, when you don't resist your desires, you take responsibility for the effect the food has on you. If you love and respect yourself, you don't want to create discomfort or self-loathing. That is part of the way you related to yourself in the past, but no longer.

We all have certain foods for which we have an intolerance or that don't agree with us, foods that have certain consequences, and yet the forbidden nature of these foods keeps us eating them. If you stop and think about what the food will feel like in your body after you've eaten it, you may want to say, "Well yes, I know I can have it, but do I really want to feel the way I know that I will feel, having eaten that cheese pizza, chocolate cupcake, pint of ice cream, etc.?" Not that there is anything wrong with the food itself. Any food can have a place in your diet. You just want to look beyond the immediate gratification of the moment, and know that the food will have an effect on you with which you have not been very pleased or happy in the past.

Part of you may say, "I don't care. I just want it." And that is the part that needs to be satisfied before you can let go of compulsive eating. Continue being gentle with yourself and relate to all of this as a learning process. Realize that you have certain thoughts and beliefs about foods, and that these relationships will not disappear overnight.

HOMEPLAY

1. What do you want?

Every time you have a wish or a brief thought about something you want, write it down immediately. Write down anything, from any area of your life, (not just body goals), no matter how outrageous or impossible it seems to you. It could be something small or large, it doesn't have to be practical at all. Don't edit yourself - write whatever you feel. It is most important to let yourself know what you want. You might review the list and determine to actually do some of the items on your list. Also, pay attention to your feelings, maybe you "wish" so and so would treat you differently or that this person were not around or maybe you want a hug or to escape work and go for a walk. Whatever it is, capture it and write it down.

Some of the things I want right now are: _____

_____

_____

2. Feelings

Take some time right now to relax and think about some of the messages you've been given and beliefs you have about emotional expression and feelings and write them down. What messages did you receive about feelings and the expression of feelings? _____

_____

_____

From your parents? _____

_____

From siblings? _____

_____

From teachers? _____

_____

From society? _____

_____

How are these messages still affecting you as an adult? _____

_____

Are you afraid to express certain feelings? _____

_____

Is it hard even to know what you are feeling? _____

_____

Are you afraid of being made fun of or criticized for what you feel? ___

_____

Do you feel you deserve to have your emotional needs met? _____
_____

Pay attention when you are interacting with others and ask yourself what messages or beliefs are playing in your head.

This Week:

Eat when you are hungry

Eat whatever you want to eat

Eat until you are satisfied

If you overeat this week, notice your thoughts and feelings about it and write them down here:.

Why did you overeat? _____

What messages do you give yourself either while you're eating or after? _____

What was going on for you before you overate? _____
_____

> YOU SHOULD NEVER TELL YOURSELF THAT YOU ARE BAD FOR EATING ANYTHING.

Can you be gentle and forgiving with yourself?

Compassion and understanding this week:

❑ None, I felt upset with myself

❑ A little, I could understand my behavior

❑ It was okay with me, I felt compassionate towards myself

❑ A lot, I felt I nurtured myself and my desires

Chapter Five
What's that Feeling?
Hunger and Emotion

You feel your emotions all over

To some extent we all have the ability to focus on and supply that which our bodies are asking for. This is one of the things we learn in order to take care of ourselves. Sometimes, somewhere along the way, our feelings get mixed up or distorted. Some feelings can be so uncomfortable that we learn to ignore them, so as not to feel the pain that is connected to them. And sometimes we get out of touch with what we really want and need, and try to fill that need with things that don't work. You can see how people become sex addicts or use shopping to try to fill a need within themselves. Most people call these feelings "urges," and go through life trying to satisfy their urges, believing that their satisfaction is what will bring them happiness. But the satisfaction of our desires are not the way to bring about lasting happiness. Rather than try to avoid the feelings, we need to change the way we relate to them so that they do not cause us discomfort, because the discomfort is what forces us into suppressing behavior like overeating.

In relation to compulsive overeating, we could use this example, someone who has unresolved feelings of guilt regarding sex may avoid being their ideal weight because they want to entirely avoid the issue of promiscuity. Looking good and getting attention may bring up such uncomfortable feelings that they use food and/or being heavy to buffer themselves from the world and literally cushion themselves from the pain of exposure.

Feelings effect you in other ways, too. Let's say your mother has always encouraged you to eat. Every time she invites you over to dinner you eat more than you want. Perhaps you are afraid that if you tell her you don't want more food, she will be upset with you, and you are afraid of her disapproval. So you continue to overeat in her presence, because of unresolved feelings, or fear. By eating more food than you would normally, you avoid the issue of your feelings about your mother.

Here's another example. If you have an argument with your mate, and you feel anger, resentment, and frustration, you might have the urge for an ice cream sundae. If you indulge in that sundae, you might never get to resolve those feelings of frustration, which you are deciding not to feel by eating the ice cream sundae. This is what I call suppressing your feelings. If you allowed yourself to experience the feelings of anger, resentment and frustration, you would be more in a position to do something about them. If you never allow yourself to experience the feelings by eating ice cream every time they come up, your feelings are dictating your actions. So the feelings never get resolved, they simply get suppressed, and are there waiting to be activated the next time your buttons get pushed.

When you are aware of the feelings, you have the option of acting on them directly to resolve and heal them. However, sometimes you don't know what the feelings are, and many compulsive overeaters feel all of their feelings as hunger, even pleasure and excitement.

You need to learn to slow down, and end the automatic habit of putting something in your mouth as soon as you feel anything, and start to distinguish between feelings of hunger and the entire range of other feelings, including: sadness, anger, boredom, lust, rage, joy, etc. Because, even though food may do a good job of temporarily suppressing or covering up other feelings, the only feeling that food can really solve is hunger.

So to learn to distinguish between hunger and the myriad of other feelings that you have throughout the day, you need to pay more attention to every feeling, exploring and allowing yourself to feel it.

Determine what it is you're hungry for, if it isn't food, you can begin to start seeking out what will really satisfy that need. But first, you need to be able to distinguish between physical hunger and emotional feelings.

Start tuning in to your body in a different way, an open and loving way, asking your body what it needs right now, and be open to any kind of an answer. Your body might say, "I need a hot bath," or "I feel like crying." It might be a mixture of feelings, something that happened that day might be affecting you, and you are experiencing emotions related to that. Of course, the feeling that is there may actually be hunger, but by slowing down and letting yourself experience whatever feelings are there, you learn to identify the feelings and not lump them all together under the heading of hunger. You may not be able to distinguish the exact feeling right away, often feelings are a mixture, but it is important to make the effort to relax and allow the feeling to be there by not being judgmental of yourself.

HOMEPLAY

1. Using Your Weight as Protection

Examine the ways in which you use extra weight as protection. Write out responses to the following statements.

1. I feel safer when I am heavier because _____

   _____

2. When I am thin I feel less safe because _____

   _____

3. In general, people treat me _____ when I'm carrying extra weight.

4. People treat me _____ when I am thin.

5. When I am smaller (or thinner)...

a. (choose the opposite sex) Men/women respond to me _____

b. (choose the same sex) Men/women respond to me _____

6. Ways in which I feel more comfortable with extra weight _____
_____

Around men? _____

Around women? _____

7. If I were thinner I would feel threatened by _____
_____

Be afraid of _____
_____

Be uncomfortable with _____
_____

2. Examining Emotional Pain

Recall and write down a time in the last week or so when you ate as a result of or to suppress emotional pain. _____

What were you afraid would happen if you allowed yourself to feel the pain, hurt, sadness _____

Were you afraid you would cry all day, sleep all day, not go to work, run out of the room screaming or that you might injure someone or yourself? _____

As a result of eating, what happened to the pain? _____

Did you forget about it? _____

Did it go away? _____

Did it get worse? _____

Did you feel better or worse afterwards? _____

Write out some alternatives for yourself for dealing with pain. For example; Find a private space and cry, hug yourself, talk to a loved one, beat a pillow, listen to your favorite music, take a bath, do some deep breathing, etc.

3. Self-examination in the mirror

This exercise is done for the purpose of learning to accept yourself, the way you are right now, as the basis for positive change. It is not done for you to compare yourself to others and end up feeling like a failure one more time. If you find yourself being negative about how you look, stop and do this at another time. Accepting yourself as you are now does not mean that you "give up," or stop trying to improve yourself, it means that you accept the reality of where you're at now. This allows you to take responsibility for your choices in the past, and start with an entirely new perspective, from today forward.

Gaze at yourself in a full-length mirror. Describe yourself, as if you were telling someone else about you. Use descriptive, non-judgmental statements, such as, "I curve here and this area goes in. I have such-and-such color eyes, and short blond hair. This area here is hard, and this area is soft." Only do this exercise if you can maintain a non-judgmental perspective. If you find yourself saying negative statements, stop and try it again another time.

Try to take some deep, relaxing breaths as you do this process and "be with" your feelings.

3. Inner Child play

Find some quiet time alone and spend time visualizing and getting to know your inner child. Find out what she feels, likes, dislikes etc. If she is upset, angry, hurt or lonely - find out why. Offer her your assistance, let her know you are there for her, reassure and comfort her.

This Week:

Eat when you are hungry

Eat whatever you want to eat

Eat until you are satisfied

If you overeat this week, notice your thoughts and feelings about it and write them down:

Why did you overeat? _____

What messages do you give yourself either while you're eating or after? _____

_____

What was going on for you before you overate? _____

Can you be gentle and forgiving with yourself? _____

Chapter Six
Changing Your Relationship to Food Forever

Feeding yourself on demand

One of the more unusual aspects of this program is that you learn to honor your own uniqueness with regard to what and when you want to eat. For a long time, you may have been making yourself rigidly conform to a diet program and schedule that is completely different from the way you really like to eat. For example, some people really aren't hungry in the morning when they wake up, but on some diet programs, you are told that you must eat breakfast whether you want to or not. The issue here is not whether breakfast is good for you, but that if you don't want it, you're not going to be successful on a diet that states you must have it. Not to mention that many of these diets don't honor the fact that we all have completely individual preferences.

When you are practicing eating whatever you want when you want, it is important to tune into your body and listen to what it is asking to be fed. If your body is asking for a hamburger and fries and you give it Caesar salad, you'll still be unsatisfied. You can never get enough of that which you don't really want. Think about this example: if you are feeling that you'd like to taste and have something in your stomach like a cheese omelet, no amount of crackers or pickles will satisfy that desire. Trying to satisfy a hunger with the wrong food will result in eating more food than is necessary, and you'll still be unsatisfied. In other words, if you're trying to satisfy yourself with something that your body isn't really hungry for, you'll eat more than you need trying to get full. If you give yourself the food that you're craving and it is exactly what you want, you will find that you will be able to eat less and be satisfied.

> IT IS VERY DIFFICULT TO ACHIEVE A POSITIVE OUTCOME FROM A NEGATIVE STANDPOINT. THE LESS ACCEPTABLE YOU FEEL YOU ARE, THE LESS ABLE YOU ARE TO MAKE POSITIVE CHANGES IN YOUR LIFE.

Eating when you're hungry, stopping when you're full

I've been asking you to eat whatever you want whenever you want it, and now I want you to start to focus on your feelings of hunger. Yes, that's right! Exactly what you've been trying to avoid feeling for so long, your hunger. Out of anxiety regarding food and eating, many people never let themselves feel hungry. Because of dieting, bingeing or compulsive eating cycles, they lose touch with their natural body rhythms of hunger and satisfaction. If you learn to listen, really tune in and feel your body, you will find that your body will tell you when you need fuel and it's time to eat. Children naturally have this ability of knowing when they are hungry and want to eat, and when they don't want to eat because they're not hungry. Dieting and compulsive overeating suppresses your natural ability to know when to feed yourself. However, these exercises allow you to start recovering that natural ability. So now, explore the idea of letting yourself get hungry before you eat and tune into the feeling.

When is the last time that you allowed yourself to feel hunger? Perhaps you would be willing to try this experiment: Instead of just putting food into your body when you're not hungry because you think you may feel hungry later, try to allow yourself to experience actual body hunger. This may be anxiety provoking for many people, but you can lessen that anxiety by reassuring yourself that you can eat anytime you want to, you're just experimenting with your feelings. As you're getting used to this idea, carry some of your favorite foods with you wherever you go to decrease your anxiety regarding hunger.

If you're feeling that familiar feeling that you usually feed to make go away, check in with your stomach and see if it's really hunger. If you think that it isn't, then don't eat, but try to see if you can tell what the feeling is. It could be nervousness over a presentation you're giving this morning, or something else that isn't really fixed by food.

If it is real stomach hunger, see how strong it is. Sometimes you're only hungry for a little something, and sometimes you may be thirsty. If you know you are feeling actual body hunger, then go ahead and have some food, whatever you think will really satisfy that hunger. You may want just a few bites of food, so eat that and check in with your body. Notice how the food tastes and feels. Be aware of how the food is making you feel when you eat it, and what your satisfaction level is. If you've established that you have a genuine hunger for food, then take a few bites and ask yourself, "Okay, now how does that feel?" Check in with your body and see if this is really the food for which you are hungry. As you feed yourself, continue to notice how it is feeling in your body. If it is exactly the food you want, have a few more bites and let yourself feel the satisfaction of feeding yourself with such delicious food. If it is not the food that you are really hungry for, reevaluate your hunger or the choice of food, or both, but if it is not delicious to you, don't continue to eat it. Eat only the best, most satisfying, finest food you can get.

Learn to pay attention when you're putting food into your body. Are you stuffing the food into your body without really tasting it because of feelings of shame or guilt? Take your time and notice what's going on with you when you're eating. Make every time you eat an exercise in expanding your awareness about your relationship to food and your body. You're worth that kind of effort, aren't you?

Don't indulge in preventative eating. That's where you eat a little (or a lot) extra now, because you might get hungry later. That's the old diet mentality. Live for the moment! Eat just enough to satisfy yourself now, knowing you can have more later, if you want more.

Using this process of feeling how hungry you are, and eating just enough to fill that hunger will put you in touch with knowing how much or how little food you actually need to feel satisfied. It will start to make you more aware of the many times that you eat for reasons other than hunger, such as social or sedative eating. Knowing this, you can make a choice whether or not you feel like accepting that second dinner at Aunt Sophie's because you're hungry or just trying to be nice.

The Hunger Scale

Here is a tool that you may find valuable in becoming more aware of just how much you need to eat. You can use an imaginary hunger scale for gauging your hunger and satisfaction levels. You can be more aware of how much food you need and be more comfortable in your body.

At **level one**, you feel really empty; you haven't eaten for hours, and there's definitely a strong, physical hunger. You're really out of fuel, and need to feed yourself. You may even feel a little lightheaded. If you've eaten a light dinner the night before, this could be your hunger level before breakfast.

Level two is when you are quite hungry, and could eat a good meal. Food is important at this level, and your thoughts about food and desire to eat are strong.

Level three would be the feeling that you could eat something, and it's easy to think of a food that would be tasty.

Level four is feeling just a little hungry, as you would an hour after eating a good meal. Food is not uppermost in your mind.

Level five is basically feeling satisfied. You don't feel hungry and you don't feel full. You experience satisfaction and that "just-right" feeling. You feel perfect with regard to your stomach. It's quite easy not to think of food at level five.

Level six is having eaten a little more that your body needs. You're not really uncomfortable, but you've satisfied your body hunger and you're slightly past the point of really wanting to eat.

At **level seven**, you begin to know that you should stop, and you start giving yourself reasons why you don't. If you stopped here, you wouldn't have to eat again for several hours.

At **level eight** you begin to feel quite uncomfortable. You know you've gone past what you need to eat to feel full, and there are other reasons that you're still putting food in your mouth.

Level nine feels as if you'll never stop eating and you hate that you are doing this to yourself. This level is painful and brings about intense self-loathing and recrimination about your body and your relationship to food.

Level ten is your worst Thanksgiving Day nightmare. You feel guilty and ashamed, as well as bloated and know you'll have a bad food hangover. You promise yourself you'll never eat this much again.

Many of us don't know how much food it actually takes to feel satisfied. This scale is used as a tool for you to help notice how hungry you are, and eat an appropriate amount. I recommend that you let yourself reach a three or two and a half before eating, and then keep assessing your feelings of fullness until you're at five, six, or six and a half. When you go to seven or beyond, you know that you're eating for reasons other than hunger. Of course, everyone overeats at times, because they've let themselves become overly hungry, or simply because the food tastes really good. However, we're not talking about stuffing yourself occasionally at a party or on Thanksgiving. It's what you do daily that is important here. If you consistently eat twenty percent beyond what your body needs to feel satisfied, you will carry around an additional twenty percent of extra weight. When you stop feeding yourself more than you need to feel satisfied, the extra weight will simply start to drop away, without any feelings of deprivation or effort at restricting your intake.

THE EATING GUIDELINES FOR LOVING YOURSELF THIN

Here are the powerful guidelines for Loving Yourself Thin. Eating in accord with these guidelines will challenge many ideas that you have regarding eating. However, using them can vastly change your relationship to food and your body will change accordingly. Refer to them whenever you eat.

> IS IT REALLY SO NECESSARY FOR EVERYONE TO CONFORM TO ONE VERY SPECIFIC IDEA OF HOW ALL BODIES SHOULD BE?

1. Eat when you feel hungry. Ask yourself: am I hungry for food, or something else?

2. Eat only what you want, and exactly what you want.

3. Eat until you are no longer hungry. Your definition of fullness may change over time. You may want to refer again to the hunger scale above.

4. Sit down and eat in a calm environment. (Usually not your car)

5. Apply your awareness to how the food tastes, feels, and is affecting your body. Pay attention to how full you feel.

6. Eat without distractions such as radio, television, books, mail, newspapers, or during intense or provocative conversation.

7. Do not change your food choices in the presence of others. Eat whatever you want to eat around anyone. (Very important.) No apologizing or explaining is necessary. If someone gets insistent that you should be dieting, say, "I'm healing my relationship to food by satisfying my cravings with the foods that allow me to feel fed." That should quiet them. If it doesn't, say "Why are you so interested in what I'm eating?"

8. Enjoy your food and focus on your pleasure.

You're not a Diet Victim

One of the benefits of feeding yourself on demand is that you learn that you can be satisfied regarding food and your body. You are the one who controls your eating, and that it is not your eating that is controlling you. Feeding yourself on demand allows you to get in touch with the old, ingrained habits and patterns that may, without your conscious knowledge or consent, be governing your actions regarding food.

To be realistic, if you're isolated at a job site, or if it's the middle of the night, you won't always be able to find and feed yourself exactly the thing that you want. Do the best you can and you can become very resourceful in giving yourself what will satisfy you. The result of this kind of self-care and self-nurturing is that you begin to feel that your needs and desires are important, and you're important enough to pay attention to them and care for yourself.

Because the ideas of dieting and deprivation are not options for you anymore, you must look for ways to make this program work. Learn to look for ways to care for yourself and to overcome feeling like a victim of your circumstances. You're not a victim. Shift your thinking from being someone who's trapped in unsatisfactory circumstances, to that of being a person who's very resourceful in taking care of themselves. You are learning a different way of caring for yourself, and feel that you're worth it. Sometimes it may take a little more effort in the way of planning for your day, but the effort will pay off in the realization that you can care of yourself in the way you most prefer, that you don't need to rely on anyone else to take care of you, and you think highly enough of yourself to do it. Doesn't that feel good?

HOMEPLAY

1. Tuning in to your internal voice

This exercise is to help you examine the internal and habitual messages you give yourself. Read the message on the left, and on the right side write down the message you hear in your head in response to this message. Keep repeating each statement until you have no more contradictory statements to write down next to each one. Pay attention to your emotions and body responses as you do this exercise.

For example: On the left, you read: "I, (your name), can say no to (someone significant in your life) without losing his/her love." You may notice that your first thought after you state this is, "But you know you'll feel guilty," or some such similar thought. So you write this down on the right. Then you repeat the statement to yourself: "I, (your name), can say no to (for example, my mother) without losing her love." Then you may hear my mind say, "But she'll be upset with me..." And you continue saying the statements to yourself and writing down your thoughts until your mind runs out of responses. Use additional sheets of paper as necessary.

THE STATEMENT

I _____, can say no to _____
without losing his/her love.

I._____ , deserve to be my ideal weight.

I._____ , deserve love in my life.

I._____ , am totally worthy to have
what I want in my life.

I._____ , am just fine as I am.

I._____ , deserve to succeed at whatever I do in life.

Make up some statements of your own about those things that are important to you.

2. Dining Experience

This week be sure to take the time at least once to have a true "dining experience." Choose a time when you can really treat yourself well, set a beautiful table, eat exactly what you want, without distractions, in harmonious surroundings. Slow down and enjoy your meal with appreciation and gusto. Remember to use the Hunger Scale above and rate your feeling of fullness from 1-10.

3. Love Letter

Imagine for a moment that you are someone else - an imaginary close friend who loves you completely and unconditionally. Write a letter which explains all the reasons behind your feelings. Why does this person love you so much? Why did this person choose you for a friend? As an example, you can use the following format, or you can create your own. This one is easy because all you need to do is fill in the blanks.

Dear _____ (Fill in your name)

Do you know how much I love you? I think you do. But do you know why I love you so dearly? Let me tell you.

I love you because _____

And also because _____

The first time I met you I knew I wanted to be your friend because:___

_____

Just being with you _____

You don't have to _____

Because you already _____

I admire you in so many ways. Here are a few of the ways I love and admire you _____

_____

Every now and then you act a little _____

But it's OK with me because I know _____

I would be afraid to be this frank with most people, but not with you because _____

_____

Your loving friend and best fan,

This Week:

Eat when you are hungry

Eat whatever you want to eat

Eat until you are satisfied

If you overeat this week, notice your thoughts and feelings about it and write them down here:.

Why did you overeat? _____

What messages do you give yourself either while you're eating or after.
_____

What was going on for you before you overate? _____

If you feel angry about eating, can you be gentle and forgiving with yourself?

CHAPTER SEVEN

Stop Being Down on Yourself - Learning Positive Self Talk

If you could really get what you want by being hard enough on yourself, everyone would have everything that they want. However, you may have noticed that beating yourself up hasn't achieved the results you have hoped for with regard to your body or weight loss. Many people think that you can create change in your body just through will power alone.

You hear things like, "Fat people just eat too much; just eat less and exercise more; the hardest exercise is pushing away from the table, etc." We've all heard these statements a hundred times, and if believing in them had worked for us, then we'd all be where we want to be, but these ideas haven't helped. However, to one degree or another, subconsciously at least, we've all bought into them. The self-contempt that you have for your body, your eating habits and your weight stems, to a large extent, from messages that you've taken in about yourself, believed and made your own.

All of us have voices inside our head that are constantly giving us messages throughout the day about all kinds of things, including our looks, what we're wearing, how we do things, how people are relating to us, and, especially if you feel that your body is not right, about your size and what you're doing about it. We're constantly judging and criticizing ourselves for being the way we are, but hardly ever praising ourselves for the good things that we are and do.

Just notice how judgmental you are of yourself and your looks the next time you look in a mirror. Having a bad hair day? See a new wrinkle or a blemish? Do you tell yourself how awful these things are? The truth is that these thoughts are not doing you any good, and in fact, they are doing you a great deal of harm. We don't really realize how powerful these negative messages are, but we end up feeling bad about ourselves because of them. The negative thoughts and messages that we give ourselves throughout the day contribute to the lack of self-esteem that we feel and decrease our ability to go after and get the things we really want in our lives. Notice if you ever have thoughts like, "If I had her body, I could get any man I want." Or, "Nobody my size ever goes skating on the boardwalk, people will laugh at me." Or "If only I was a size 8, I could wear great clothes and look good."

It's not your fault

There was a time when you naturally and spontaneously accepted the body that you have. Although you started out innocent, at some point you looked in the mirror, and said, "I don't look like I should. My body is not acceptable to me. I am not right." Where did these thoughts and ideas about yourself come from? You didn't come up with these ideas on your own. There were stimuli outside yourself that gave you the idea that your body wasn't okay. Being a member of a family, or a group, or our society, you are conditioned by it and your values and ideals are mostly shaped mostly by forces outside yourself. It's not your fault, but you are at the effect of these ideals. Your dissatisfaction with your body size or shape came from messages you received from family, society, and the media about how you should be.

Some ideas come from our families. If someone has been critical of you in the past for being overweight, and that person's opinion is important to you, you "internalize" their way of thinking and accept it as your own. Perhaps you did not even agree with them. "Well," you think, "if Mommy thinks I'm too fat, then I guess I am." You are innocent and impressionable, and a part of you also adopts the idea that you're too fat.

Some ideas come from the media. When you see only images of slender women as being objects of love and desire, then you naturally surmise that to be desirable, you must be slender. You're constantly being told that thin is better and that eating is somehow awful and shameful, especially for fat people. Even though you're constantly getting thin messages, you can also realize that these messages are not your ideas, they were learned. You can assert that you do not accept that thinness is the only appropriate way to be and that dieting is the only way to achieve your ideal body. You can come to believe in and assert a viewpoint that is more appropriate for you. Is it really so necessary for everyone to conform to one very specific idea of how all bodies should be?

If you can look at some of the awful ways that you treat yourself for being overweight, you can realize that beating yourself up about the way you look does nothing to help you and that this self-abuse is harmful to your self-esteem. You keep telling yourself that if you're tough enough and discipline yourself enough, then the latest fad diet will work for you. But it doesn't make sense to expect to achieve a positive outcome by forcing yourself to diet because you see yourself as wrong the way you are. By making yourself and your body wrong, you just feel worse, and in the long run, using negativity to motivate yourself never works.

You deserve to eat, just like everyone

Have you ever noticed feeling ashamed of your appetite and desire to eat? Do you feel that people are judging you regarding your body size and your food choices? There is a very pervasive sense in our society that you are not allowed to eat if your body size exceeds the popular ideal. Start to become aware of these thoughts and feelings when you are eating in the presence of others, in a social situation or even at the checkout counter at the market. Rebel against accepting these ideas! The shame that you feel about eating was a learned response. You didn't suddenly start disliking yourself because of your size. At some point you accepted the constant input of others who, for reasons of their own, felt that your size wasn't acceptable.

In our society, people will tend to judge you based on your size, that seems to be a fact of life. But you needn't allow this to dictate and the way you feel about yourself and your food choices. Allowing yourself to be dictated to is an extension of your desire to please others with your personal appearance, and you must assert to yourself and others that you deserve to be whoever you are, exactly as you are right now. To counter these feelings that you don't deserve to eat, tell yourself continually that you are a worthwhile human being, no matter what your size. After all, if you were to lose weight, you would still have the same idiosyncrasies and quirks that you have at your present size. Doesn't it make sense that you also have the same strengths and wonderful qualities now? You're the same person. You won't be any more fun, loving, smarter or savvy when you lose weight, you'll just be thinner. Recognize that you have the same qualities right now that you would have if you were to lose weight, and start appreciating yourself now!

By doing this, you can start to live your life based on your strengths. Then, if you feel a desire to make a change, that is a decision for self-improvement, and you will be more motivated to do whatever it takes. You're motivated from a place of feeling okay the way you are, not the feeling that you must change to be okay with yourself and society. You're making a change because it's the next thing you feel like tackling, like mastering a martial art, or learning pottery. Your self-esteem doesn't need to be dependent on your size, and you could see changing your body as an interesting challenge.

Get rid of your scale

The next step in eliminating negative self-talk is to get rid of one of the worst perpetrators: your bathroom scale. The purpose of this is to help you remove the obsessive focus on your body size, based on a number. The scale keeps you focused on a number as a measure of your self-esteem – another aspect of the diet mentality. "150 lbs. is better that 160 lbs...110 lbs. is better than 112," and so forth. Where does it end? If losing is good, then gaining is bad, and this wreaks havoc on your self esteem. If one week you're a good person based on what you ate, are you a bad person the next week if you gained weight? The point is that we don't think, "Oh, I'm a little heavier this week, because I've been eating more. So what?" We take it personally and extend the idea that we're a diet failure into every aspect of our lives and demoralize ourselves because of the one issue: we haven't been eating in alignment with our body goals.

So if you've ever experienced five pounds of metal and glass ruining your entire day, you're allowing this inanimate, mechanical object to dictate how you feel about yourself, based on the number you see. You may wake up in the morning feeling light, lean and good about yourself, and then you step on the scale and discover, to your horror, that you're actually two pounds heavier. You feel defeated and depressed when you were feeling great to begin with. All of us fluctuate two or three pounds on a daily basis depending on such things as water retention, hormonal cycles and how full your colon is. So to allow the scale to dictate to you how you will feel about yourself is giving up your power to this object. You're giving it the power to make you have a good or bad day, based on something which naturally fluctuates.

Some people tell me that they're afraid that if they don't have the scale as an alarm to show them they're gaining weight, they'll just continue to gain and get completely out of control. They think that a constant reminder that they haven't reached their goal is a good motivator. In the long run, the scale itself doesn't help you achieve your goals. Quite the contrary, on a day to day basis, it serves to make you a lot more miserable, because it's a constant reminder of your failure.

Be a friend to yourself

Take back control of how you feel about yourself! Make the decision that you're not going to make yourself unhappy and start to wean yourself off weighing in on a daily basis. You will begin to know when you start losing weight by the way your clothes and body look and feel. It's best if you can stop weighing yourself entirely. What difference does it really make if you weigh 180 or 183, if you are unhappy at either weight?

As you learn the tools of Loving Yourself Thin and start putting them into practice, your body will begin to change. Your focus will not be so obsessive about your weight and it is common for people to drop five or ten pounds before they realize it. Of course, something will be changing about your eating habits and your relationship to food, and you will be quite aware of that.

If you must diet, diet from Negative Self-Talk

Think about the kind of boss for whom you are most motivated to do a good job: one who yells at you and berates you for what a bad job you are doing, one who constantly causes you stress by telling you how wrong you are, as opposed to one who approaches you with understanding and compassion, and lets you know that you are doing well, or at least acknowledges that you are trying. If you've ever had someone in your life who's constantly on your back about something, you'll probably remember that you wanted to change that behavior less or not at all. It seems that there is something in the human psyche that makes us feel rebellious toward even the discipline we try to give ourselves. Maybe it's a carry over from childhood, but if you're constantly beating yourself up and telling yourself that you're bad, and that your body is wrong, there's this rebellious part of you that says, "I'll show you. I won't let you change, no matter what," isn't there? So you can see that continually beating yourself up about your eating habits and your weight doesn't promote change, doesn't promote self-love, and hasn't given you your ideal body.

A very powerful aspect of Loving Yourself Thin process is to start to be aware of the voice inside your head telling you that you're not okay the way you are. Pay attention to it, and start changing those negative messages to positive ones. This is very important. We all do it, and you need to start recognizing that those negative statements are harming you. When you hear that little voice inside your head, whatever the message is, be compassionate with yourself regarding that statement. For example, you might hear yourself say,"You know that was bad for you. Why can't you control yourself more?" Or, as you're getting dressed for your day or evening, and you look in the mirror and say, "I look disgusting, just look at my stomach. I hate my body!" If you catch yourself starting to say these negative statements, stop and say, "Whoa! That may have been so in the past, and that might be what I used to think, but I'm not going to get down on myself for that today. This is the first day of loving myself thin and I think that things are going to be different for me now." The whole point is to be aware of the negative statements that you say about yourself, set them aside, and affirm the positive. How do you do that? Well, read on…

Change comes from a place of positivity

Many people think that by being hard on ourselves, we can make ourselves reach our goals. Think about some of the mean things that you've done to yourself when you've been dieting in the past. Have you ever put a picture of yourself at your heaviest on the refrigerator door, thinking that if you get disgusted enough, you'll stop overeating? Have you ever worn clothes that are uncomfortable and too tight, with the idea that it will serve as a reminder to not eat as much? Have you refused to go out and buy new clothes in a larger size that actually fit, because you didn't want to accept the fact that you had gained weight? Pause for a moment and reflect on how well these methods have worked for you.

It is very difficult to achieve a positive outcome from a negative standpoint. The more unacceptable that you feel you are, the less able you are to make positive changes in your life, because you feel weak and victimized. The more that you accept and acknowledge yourself and affirm that you're already okay the way you are, the more able you will be to create lasting changes in your life. Slowly and surely, you are going to start to replace those negative self-abuse messages with powerful and positive thoughts of self-love and support.

Don't expect yourself to arrive instantly at a place of total self love and acceptance, because the negative messages you have been habitually giving yourself are powerful and pervasive. Just remember that habits can be changed by being aware of what you are doing and gently coach yourself into a more accepting space. Start to shift the focus of the messages you hear yourself saying. Instead of , "I hate my body, I hate the way I look, I think I'm ugly," you can say, "Okay, this is my body now and I accept that maybe my body is not exactly where I want it to be, or look how I think it should look, but I'm taking care of myself and moving to a place of greater love and acceptance, and doing things to feel better about my body." You don't have to say that you think your body is perfect the way that it is, or even say you absolutely love your body, although that's wonderful if you can. It's good enough for you to change the message from one of "I hate it," to one of "I'm okay, this is where my body is now and I'm taking care of myself and working toward changing myself." This doesn't mean being totally unrealistic, but when you find yourself looking in the mirror and thinking, "I hate my body, look at those fat rolls and those ugly thighs …" just stop yourself and say "Stop that. I like my chest and I like my face, and I'm not so happy with the way my legs look right now, but I'm willing to make a change, and I'm working on feeding myself and taking care of myself." Then when you are able to, go on to give yourself messages like, "I'm happy that I have this body, it's served me well in my life. I like this or that about myself, I'm really okay." Later on, when it seems appropriate to you, you can give yourself wonderful, loving and positive messages like, "I love everything about my body, I'm a beautiful person from head to toe, I look great, I'm so lucky to have a healthy body to live in," and other statements like these that you will be happy to create yourself.

It's very important to pay attention to the messages you give yourself, and creates a very powerful sense of well-being when you can affirm the positive and nurture yourself. If you can encourage yourself, take it easy on the negative self-talk, and empower yourself in the ways that you're eating and living, then you're in a stronger position to create a better situation in your life and with your body. The more you can relax and accept yourself being okay exactly the way you are, the less you will have to use food to suppress your uncomfortable emotions about disliking yourself. If you accept yourself as you are now, it's much easier to change. So more and more, every time you catch yourself saying a negative message, turn it around and affirm the positive about that thought. See if you can accept the opposite of the negative statement you just made about yourself. It took a long time and much negative conditioning to build up the self-hatred that you feel for your body, and it's not your fault. If you remember your original innocence, and that you believed those negative messages because it seemed like the right idea at the time, it will help you to start letting go and give yourself messages of love and acceptance.

Self-acceptance vs. resignation

Many people have the idea that by accepting themselves the way they are right now, they are "giving up", or resigning themselves to being overweight forever. "If I just accept myself as I am now, what will be my motivation to change?" they ask. It is a feeling that most people want to avoid because of past experiences of giving up and being left with feelings of helplessness and despair. Their experience with self-acceptance is based on a negative context, that of giving up and accepting things the way they are, with no hope and no tools for change. It's usually accompanied with self-loathing because of past failures. And that's the end of their excursion into self-improvement.

When you give up, you think in a resigned way,"This is just the way it is, and it will never be any different." The basis of this thinking lies in the idea that you have to change to be okay. Resignation is a form of despairing that the future will be the same as the past.

But what if you could change your thinking and think of yourself as okay the way you are, even though you may not have your perfect body? Then making changes becomes something you've decided to do, an adventure and a challenge, based on your desires for yourself, and what's important to you.

Thinking you're okay as you are and desiring to make a change represents a shift of context regarding how you relate to yourself. You could think of self-acceptance as simply recognizing the reality of what's happening right now, without judgement. That is, you have the body you do, and certain things have contributed to that. It's not right or wrong, it's just the way it happens to be. And, that doesn't mean that it must be that way forever. If you can remove the shame and disappointment in yourself, you can see that by just acknowledging that reality gives you a new place from which to start in your process. You can think of yourself as being in a process of change, and that idea keeps you from feeling stuck in helplessness. Even though you may not yet be seeing outward manifestations of weight loss, you are changing from the inside out, and the first change is that of being positive about yourself.

Every day is an opportunity to make choices which will either carry you further toward your goal, or help you to learn something about yourself. So, as long as you are engaged in the process of learning about what makes you tick, clarifying your values, and becoming healthier, it could never be seen as simply "giving up." As we've noted, if negativity were a good motivator, the most negative people would be the most successful, and it just isn't so. Begin to face your challenges with a new positivity, expecting things to work out for your benefit, and see how that helps change your attitude about your body. Know that your body has served you, and begin to love yourself based on that fact. It will help you to have more confidence in your ability to achieve your ideal body.

HOMEPLAY

1. Alternatives for dealing with pain

This week, whenever you find yourself wanting to eat as a result of emotional pain, distress, anxiety, anger, depression, loneliness or other non-hunger reason, stop and ask yourself whether eating will take the pain away or make you feel better. Look and see if there are alternative ways that you can nurture yourself. Use the list below or write one of your own (carry it with you) and whenever you find yourself reaching for food as comfort - pull out the list. Try at least one alternative to eating and then decide if you still want to eat.

- Clean out your desk, answer correspondence
- Take a walk
- Ride stationary exercise bike
- Call someone on the phone
- Play with dog or take dog for a walk
- Clean house: vacuum, laundry, clean windows
- Organize closets, give away discards
- Rent a movie and invite a friend over to watch
- Go for a drive
- Read a book or magazine
- Go out to a movie
- Go shopping/ go to the mall
- Go to a hobby store and buy a new project to start or just look around

- Start an art project or continue an ongoing one such as: crochet an afghan or paint a still life
- Visit a friend or family member
- Go to the park
- If you are upset with someone, confront them
- Meet new people through the Internet
- Scream into a pillow, cry or beat a pillow
- Go to sleep or take a nap
- Make gift lists, start Christmas shopping early
- Set up a budget
- Update your resume
- Find volunteer work
- Look in the classified ads for a second income
- Organize income tax paperwork for this year's return
- Start a major project such as furniture painting
- Go to the animal shelter and give the animals love and attention
- Go to a pet store
- Get the car washed or wash and polish it yourself
- Snuggle with someone you love to snuggle with
- Do deep breathing or visualizations
- Write in your journal or write a story or song
- Make a list of all the things you have to be grateful for
- Do affirmations
- Go to a card shop - buy and send cards just for fun
- Go to a toy store
- Write a letter
- Do all the errands you've been putting off: get gas in the car, have duplicate keys made, shoe repair, dry cleaners, post office, alterations,

oil changed in car, etc.
- Go to a book store and browse
- Go for a hike in the hills
- Play video games
- Drive to the beach
- Give the dog a bath
- Condition your hair
- Get a pedicure
- Schedule a massage, ask for or trade a massage
- Give yourself a massage
- Play music or dance
- Water and care for plants
- Go to the gym
- Get a facial or give yourself one
- Make a "wish list" collage: perfect figure, great trips, romance, wealth, etc.
- Rollerskate
- Pluck eyebrows
- Pray
- Go to the zoo
- Play solitaire
- Go look at models of new homes
- Look through and/or organize photo albums
- Organize a group going to Disneyland
- Balance your checkbook
- Try a new hairstyle
- Create a scrapbook
- Buy a new address book and transfer numbers

- Buy wallpaper stencils and paint and apply to room
- Ask a friend to join you in going to a swap meet
- Go the library or a museum
- Soak in a jacuzzi
    - Borrow a kid and play
    - Go to a travel agency and get brochures on dream vacations
    - Listen to subliminal tapes
    - Drink water
    - Write a love letter to yourself
    - Do yoga

> WOULDN'T YOU RATHER BE FRIENDS WITH YOUR BODY THAN CONSTANTLY BATTLING YOURSELF?

2. Deep Breathing/Ideal Self Imaging

At least two or three times over the next week take the time to sit down and do the following deep breathing/ideal self imaging exercise. If you feel ambitious, make a tape of the questions with pauses after each, so you can really concentrate on your inner experience as you do this exercise.

Sit down and take some deep breaths, and relax as you exhale. Imagine in your mind's eye how you would look if you had your ideal body. See how your hair would look, and your face. Look down and see how your body looks and how you are dressed. Notice every curve and area of your body. spend a few minutes looking at the various parts of yourself, really getting a clear picture of your ideal body.

Imagine yourself in different situations with your ideal body, looking really great. Your hair is wonderful, your clothes are just right and your body is just the way you want it to be. Imagine yourself in a family situation, seeing members of your family and your friends. How are they responding to you and you to them? Include your mother, father, siblings, old boyfriends or girlfriends, and anybody who may have been unkind to you in the past.

Do you feel good, or are you feeling arrogant or superior? Are you incurring the jealousy of anyone? What are people saying to you? How do you feel?

Change the setting and see yourself with your ideal body at work. How are your co-workers responding to you? What kind of comments are you receiving? How does this feel to you?

Imagine yourself in an intimate situation, with a lover or spouse. How are they responding to you and you to them? Does this feel comfortable or threatening?

Spend some time examining what life will be like as your ideal self. What are you feeling? How are people responding? How can you make it more OK for your ideal self to exist?

This Week:

Eat when you are hungry

Eat whatever you want to eat

Eat until you are satisfied

If you overeat this week, notice your thoughts and feelings about it and write them down here:

Why did you overeat? _____

What messages do you give yourself either while you're eating or after?_____

_____

What was going on for you before you overate? _____

Can you be gentle and forgiving with yourself?

CHAPTER EIGHT

When Fat's "Where It's At": How Compulsive Eating is a Way to Avoid Other Issues

Getting in touch with how your weight and preoccupation with food serves you brings an interesting awareness to the situation. Food is a wonderful coping mechanism. It is a way to combat boredom and treat yourself. Perhaps you use food to alleviate anxiety and keep the harsh world at bay. Talking about the latest diets and your struggle with your weight can create a wonderful bonding atmosphere, because so many people can relate to it. This doesn't make food wrong, and it doesn't make you wrong that you use food to relieve stress or other reason, but now that you are ready to make changes in your life and eating habits, it is beneficial to acknowledge this and move on. Some people use alcohol or drugs. They are all means of coping and some are more destructive than others.

Taking responsibility for all of your choices, in every area of your life, means that you can applaud yourself for your desire to find other, healthier ways of coping than using food to solve life's problems.

When fat's where it's at...

You may not want to acknowledge this, but sometimes you continue to keep on extra pounds because there is some kind of payoff for you. We may all have different reasons, but there may be reasons that you choose to hold on to your weight. Staying fat may actually have its benefits and work better for you. If you find yourself reacting against this idea, just try to stay open-minded about and notice if any of the following situations ring true for you:

- If you've been overweight for a long time, you may have gotten much negative attention from your family and friends for it, and perhaps negative attention being better than no attention at all, you've kept weight on for fear of losing the attention that you do get.

- If your parents or spouse were constantly telling you to lose weight, your keeping weight on may be your statement that you won't be told what to do, even if it might benefit you. Is your weight the symbol of a power struggle between you and someone else, a "screw you" to someone who wants to make you change? It may be a visible statement of "I'm going to be however I want to be, no matter what you say."

* You may have fears about making changes, or a desire to avoid exchanging unknown problems for the ones you're familiar with.

- If you had your ideal body, would you create disapproval from friends, and/or relatives? Are you keeping extra weight on because you're afraid of making people jealous, or having other people think you're "stuck-up?"

- If you had your ideal body, do you think you would be unbearably arrogant?

- Were you rewarded with food a lot as a child, or were you a fussy eater? Did your parents encourage you to eat and praise you when you did? We have all heard of the starving children in China or wherever our parents felt would be the place most likely to get us to clean our plates, did your parents reward you for being captain of the Clean Plate Club?

- Are you continuing to be "good," and please your parents when it no longer has any bearing on your relationship?

- If you just dream about being your ideal size and never experience the reality of it, you can indulge in unfounded fantasies about how your life would be if you were your ideal weight. In never finding out what life would be like, you can allow yourself all these fantasies, which are probably better than reality.

- Your sense of yourself as a powerful person might be connected to your large size, and there might be a fear of losing that sense. You feel more important when you are able to "throw some weight around." Some people fear being thin, weak, vulnerable, "thin-skinned." Being lighter makes them feel the slings and arrows of the world too intensely. Keeping extra weight on may actually make a lot of sense if you felt this way about yourself, wouldn't it?

- As you approach the entire arena of relationships and sex, you have a rich diversity of reasons. For example, if you don't have confidence in your ability to say "no" to unwanted advances, staying fat is a good way to avoid the issue entirely. Extra weight is also used as a barrier to keep attention away from you, to attempt to make yourself invisible, or to add an extra layer of insulation against unwanted glances or remarks. If this resonates with you, think about whether your strategy is really working. There are many very beautiful, large women who get a lot of attention. Does the extra weight really achieve your purpose? Doesn't it make more sense to heal the feelings related to being seen or appreciated, than it does to try to hide behind a wall of weight?

More reasons that fat may be better for you than thin...

- Another reason: if you were to think of yourself as sexy and desirable, you may fear being too promiscuous. Keeping the extra weight on can be a form of self-punishment or guilt from having had an affair. If you have a jealous mate, and fear confronting that issue, extra weight can be a means of guaranteeing that you won't be "too attractive."

- Something else regarding relationships: everyone wants to be loved for themselves, and what better way to test a partner's love than to keep unwanted pounds on and make sure they love you for your "real self?"

- You might have a fear of success, a fear of being too visible in your career and getting too much attention. If you don't have the self-esteem to accept compliments graciously, the extra weight may keep the compliments away. I don't know how many times I've heard women tell me that, after dieting, they had a lot of people tell them how great they look. Not being able to accept the appreciation of others, or feeling too exposed, they slowly and surely gain back all the weight they'd lost. Then they hate themselves, not recognizing that the weight serves to protect them from emotional situations with which they weren't comfortable.

• As odd as it may seem, some people have the fear that they will not have anything to occupy their time, or problems to solve. Other people may be reluctant to give up the struggle with their bodies and their weight, thinking that there will be a vacuum in their lives, nothing to deal with. These last two ideas are subconscious, of course, but still operate as a dynamic in keeping on weight.

When confronted with all of the issues that one uses food to avoid, it's easy to see how a person could want to avoid the issue of being smaller altogether, preferring to keep the problems they have rather than exchanging them for "new" problems. "At least they're MY problems, and I know what to expect."

EXERCISE

Here's an exercise to help you learn more about the reasons you may be carrying around extra weight. If you feel that you really don't need to do this part, notice if you feel like avoiding thinking about these things, and really be open to gaining some beneficial insights regarding your relationship to your body and weight. You probably need to confront these feelings in yourself.

Write down your responses to the following questions and statements as they occur to you. Write as much or as little as you like, but try to be as honest with yourself as you can. It is beneficial to write your responses quickly, without too much intellectual censoring, and then go back and review your responses more thoughtfully. Be open to surprising yourself with your answers.

1. One of the things that compulsive overeating helps me avoid is _____

_____

2. Another thing that compulsive overeating helps me avoid is_____

_____

3. Some fears I have about giving up overeating and/or losing weight are _____

_____

4. Some of the fears that I have about being my ideal weight are_____

_____

5. Do you feel that extra weight protects you from unwanted or painful sexual encounters?

_____

6. Have there been circumstances in your past that are too painful to live with at your thinner, ideal weight? _____

_____

Taking your life off hold...

Another interesting belief system that operates for people who are overweight, or have a negative body image even at normal weight, is that once they get their ideal body, their lives will start. They keep their lives on hold, and never do the things they really love or go after the things that would bring them real satisfaction, because they feel their body isn't right. This allows them to live in the realm of fantasy, without ever making the effort to achieve their dreams. "My life hasn't started yet, because I'm fat," the thinking goes, "but as soon as I'm thin, my life will be really good, I'll have the relationship I want and I'll be more successful in my career, or I'll get the part I want, or run the marathon." You make your current life wrong and blame it on the fact that you're overweight. You avoid doing the sports you love because you think people will be looking at us because of your size, or avoid getting into an intimate relationship because you'll have to bare your body, and that thought scares you.

You avoid these things because you're uncomfortable with yourself. You don't have a way to deal with the feelings that these experiences bring up. You feel that your life would change if only you could change your body. There are many ways in which you put your life on hold because of your current shape. Think for a moment about the things you avoid because you feel that your size or shape isn't right. What have you put off for when you finally lose those 20 pounds? Wouldn't it be a shame to go through life never having the relationship you want because you believe that you need to lose a few pounds before you can think of yourself as desirable and available?

The really unfortunate mindset that this creates is that dieting is the answer to solving all of your problems. This kind of thinking is a way to avoid the unhappiness with your life and the emotional issues that you don't want to confront. You blame it all on your weight, and believe that dieting is the means to change that. But as you've probably seen, dieting doesn't work, and even if you do manage to lose the weight, your emotional issues are still there, and perhaps you feel them even more strongly. So you probably gain the weight back and get lost in the vicious cycle of blame your weight, diet, lose weight, feel unstable, gain weight, feel like a failure, hate yourself, blame the weight, etc.

The Way Out

In chapter seven, we looked at the idea of accepting yourself the way you are right now, as a means to become the person you want to be. What if you were to feel that you could have the life you want, as you are now? Start looking at the things that you want in your life and begin to find ways of creating them at your present weight. Yes, right now.

Why not? If you feel too shy to go after getting a companion or lover, you'll still feel shy when you are thin. Do what it takes to resolve the emotions that keep you from having the relationship you want, and then go after it.

People tell me, "Oh, no man/woman would be interested in me at the weight I am now." Well, that's simply not true. Anyone can have fulfilling and exciting relationships if they believe they can. Look around and you'll see that many larger people have friends, lovers, husbands and wives. You need to change the way that YOU think and feel about yourself, and people will start to perceive you differently. When you start loving and appreciating yourself more for your unique beauty, talents and strength, you'll be surprised at how differently other people relate to you. They'll start finding things to appreciate about you that they have never noticed before, simply because you are projecting a different self-image, one that says, "Yes, I AM an exceptional person, a treasure trove of uniqueness, including love, humor, compassion and strength. I value myself as a complete human being."

As you begin to value yourself as a whole person, with all your unique resources, idiosyncrasies and human qualities, you can feel attractive, whatever your weight. If you value these things in yourself, your self-esteem will rise. If your self-esteem rises, you will love yourself at any weight. Perhaps your motivation to reach your ideal weight will be strengthened. Or perhaps your excess weight will matter less to you. Certainly if you love and value yourself, your weight will not be an impediment to a relationship.

Stop blaming your weight for not doing what you love or going after what you want. If you lack the motivation or perseverance to learn a new sport at your present weight, what will change if you were to lose weight? The emotions will still be there at your smaller size, so why not just go after what you want right now? Life will always be made up of large and small challenges, start tackling the ones you can handle now and go on the the larger ones.

Dreaming

Sit back and relax for a moment and think about what you would do or do differently if weight were not an issue for you. What kinds of things would you want to do in your life, even if you could never change your body size?

Would you join a social club, go square dancing, bungee-jump?

What activities would you like to participate in if you were your ideal weight?

What else might change for you and how?

What are some of the things you wish for at your ideal size?

If you were your ideal weight, would you actually go after them?

Objectification = dehumanization

YOU are not your body, your body is a part of you. Many people have come to view their bodies as ornamental, rather than as the instruments through which we act, feel and live. These women and men feel that their value as a person comes from having an attractive body, and that if their body doesn't fit well into our cultural aesthetic, which is arbitrary and changing, they lose value as an individual. Observe people on the streets and see how many of them fit into what is essentially the cultural fashion of being reed thin and/or v-shaped muscular. It is a marketing and advertising triumph that we all want to look like fashion models in a genetically varied world.

Why are we so obsessed about body types? What is wrong with having a variety of sizes? It seems that our society conditions us to view ourselves in this way. Susan Kano, author of *Making Peace with Food*, states: "It is only through extensive and continual conditioning that an intelligent human being comes to see herself as an ornament, whose first priority is the attainment of a slender body, rather than as a complete human being who has a myriad of other concerns and unlimited potential." Powerful, isn't it? It serves to remind us of how much focus and energy we have been placing on having a perfect body instead of a balanced existence. There are so many ways in which we can contribute, stop using weight and body size as a measure of value, for yourself and others.

Beauty is not only what our society defines it to be and there are many ways of learning to value yourself as an individual. Figure out ways of valuing yourself for who you are, based on your resources and strengths. Feeling good about yourself absolutely has to come from the inside out. No matter how perfect you make yourself, if your self-esteem is based on your looks, the simple inevitability of aging will undo you.

Begin to notice and reject in thought, word and action the destructive social prescription to be as thin as possible. Replace "fatism" with respect for people regardless of size. Notice when you make snap decisions about people regarding their size, and gently remind yourself that everyone has wonderful and not-so-wonderful qualities, just like you. You are as rough on yourself in your judgment as you are on other people, so try to be easier and more gentle in your thinking.

Notice how your judgmental or competitive thoughts isolate you from others. Broaden your ability to appreciate and see the beauty in all those around you, regardless of size, including yourself. Start to think of your body as both a trusted friend and a treasured home for you to enjoy and use fully, not dependent on your weight, rather than as an object to be admired or judged.

Exercise

Objectification of yourself and others

Write down any thoughts and feelings in response to the following questions.

Do you objectify others? That is, do you judge people based on their appearance alone?

_____

How much do you judge yourself on the basis of your appearance? ___

_____

Do you respect fat people less than thin people? _____

If so, does this seem fair and ethical? _____

Do you remember an occasion you were initially critical of someone and it turns out later that you really like them because they were a wonderful and interesting person? _____

_____

What helped you get around your first impression? _____

Notice the thoughts you have when you are around people at a mall or restaurant.

Are you constantly evaluating, judging and comparing? _____

Do you say things about other people that you wouldn't want said about yourself? _____

_____

How does objectifying others affect you? How does objectifying others lead to judging yourself based only on your appearance? _____

_____

Do you believe that you would be a better person or have more determination to achieve your goals if you were thinner? Why or why not? _____

Does your behavior change depending on your weight? In what ways?_

_____

Make a list of what you like about yourself and your recent accomplishments which have nothing to do with your appearance. ___

_____

_____

_____

Homeplay

We all know the disadvantages of being fat or having constant problems with our weight and eating. What may be less obvious are the benefits you get out of having this problem.

1. What are the benefits of fat/weight and having an issue with food? Consider issues such as getting attention from a doting parent who is constantly concerned about your well-being and is always after you to lose weight; or keeping away the opposite sex because you don't feel that you can handle someone's advances. _____

_____

_____

_____

2. What are your payoffs? Write down all the ways in which fat and food issues have served you, the purpose or value of them in your life, and the good reasons you have for not giving these up. _____

_____

_____

Example:

Weight or issues with food may:

...serve to keep people who aren't interested in the "real" you away.

...allow you to avoid relationships which you think may be scary and painful to you.

...keep you from confronting more serious issues that you don't want to deal with.

...keep you from confronting your fear of success or failure.

...be your excuse for not doing/having what you want.

...provide you with a sense of security, safety and power.

Some of the things that my struggling with my weight may helps me avoid are:

2. From Resentment to Self-assertion

Overweight people often put others' desires before theirs and then resent it. In order for you to lessen feelings of resentment when you feel others are making overwhelming demands on you, begin to notice if you put others' needs or demands before your own. This week, whenever you have a problem with someone requesting your time or resources, take the following steps. First, clarify the problem. For example, if your boss/child/spouse wants something done right away and you feel you do not have the time, ask if they will discuss it for a moment. Determine exactly what they need and whether it must be done today and by you. Explain your problem with meeting their request and propose an alternate solution, perhaps someone else might do it or you might do it tomorrow. Maybe the priorities of your tasks could be rearranged. If the problem is urgent and you are the only one that can do the particular task, perhaps someone else could do one of the other things you were going to do. Define the problem, review the options and find a solution that works for both of you. It takes practice and willingness for people to learn to consistently take themselves and others into account when solving problems. Honor your feelings and let it be known that your desires are as important as anyone else's.

2. Relaxing in the Face of Fear

Whenever you are experiencing a thought or fear related to your weight or body issues that is making you uncomfortable and creating anxiety and worry, stop and take a moment and review that thought. For example, "I'm fat and I'm afraid of so-and-so or my family seeing me like this." Acknowledge that you feel this way. "I feel uncomfortable seeing _____ at my present weight." Recognize that your body is as it is right now. Nurture yourself by saying, "OK, this is how my body is, I am not going to be 10 lbs. thinner by tomorrow. Panic and worry are not going to be of any use in changing that. So I choose to accept myself as I am." Assume the positive. Know that you are working toward healing yourself and that takes time. You can't be any better in the moment than you are. accept that you're in a process of change for the better, and that's good enough. Let go of the fear, acknowledge where you are, and the positive direction in which you are focused with your food/weight issue. Change will take time and self-acceptance is part of the process.

3. Imagining Your Ideal Self

Sit down in a quiet place and do some deep breathing to help you relax your mind.

(Again, if you're feeling ambitious and really want to get into this, a tape is a good tool to make for yourself. Just be sure to leave pauses in the dialogue to give yourself time to create the mental picture.)

Create a picture of your ideal self in your mind's eye, complete with the perfect hairstyle, makeup, and outfit. Imagine yourself in different situations as your ideal self, exactly as you would look and act if you had the body, looks, hair, face, clothes, etc. that you wish for. Spend some time examining what life will be like as your ideal self. This can be a really powerful exercise, so don't rush through it without getting the full benefit.

What are you feeling? How are people responding? Examine your feelings and write down your responses to the following people and situations if you were your ideal self;

- Career - co-workers, boss, colleagues
- Social - peers, friends
- Family - mother, father, siblings, relatives
- Relationships - sexual, non-sexual
- Dreams - doing the things you wish for yourself

What are the ways that can you make it more okay for your ideal self to exist? (For example: dealing with fears of what people will think of you, making someone wrong by being "too" gorgeous, dealing with fears of promiscuity)

This Week:

Eat when you are hungry

Eat whatever you want to eat

Eat until you are satisfied

If you overeat this week, notice your thoughts and feelings about it and write them down.

Why did you overeat? _____

What messages do you give yourself either while you're eating or after? _____

_____

Can you be gentle and forgiving with yourself?

Chapter Nine
Getting Rid of Excess Emotional Baggage

Relating to your feelings in a new and different way with Vivation®

Up until now, I have been talking about your feelings and how they can affect your behavior regarding food. I'd like to start now to give you some tools to begin the healing process, so that you are better able to address and resolve the negative emotional issues in your life.

Many people feel they would be in a better position to control their weight if they could control their feelings. By learning Vivation, you no longer need to control your feelings or emotions, because you will learn to experience your emotions in a very different way, a way that adds to your overall sense of well-being, rather than detracting from it. You can learn to turn obstacles into opportunities; take the lemons that life gives you and make lemonade. You can relate to your feelings in such a different way that they no longer bother you or cause you to act in ways that might be working against you.

By learning how to change your relationship to your feelings, you can create what we call "integration" of the feeling, that is, learning to shift how you relate to that feeling from a negative context to a positive context. (For our purposes, we are using the word "context" to mean "how you look at something," "point of view," or "attitude.") Integration is the realization that a feeling that you previously held as being negative or bad in some way can be beneficial and/or pleasurable. By being able to integrate your emotions, you learn how to eliminate internal conflicts, and become happier and more powerful. You learn that there are always unlimited choices about how you relate to a situation, when previously you thought that there is only one way to think about it. This puts you in a position to actually do something about the situation. Rather than feel helpless and victimized, you recognize that you are the one who creates what you experience in your life.

Content and context

In every experience there is a physical part and an emotional part. The physical part is the thing itself, what is happening in the moment, and we call that part the "content." For example, your being the middle child is the content of your birth order, a basic fact. The emotional part of being the middle child is the way you feel about it, good or bad. We call this part the "context." A negative context is any context in which you are comparing what is real (the actual content of a situation) to an imaginary standard and deciding that what you're imagining is better that what is real. The situation is something that in fact could be either good or bad, depending on how you look at it, and you are choosing to look at it in a way that makes it seems bad. In other words, when you hold something in a negative context, you are "making it wrong," which causes you to have certain feelings or reactions in your body.

On the other hand, a positive context is one in which you accept what is actually happening, rather than comparing it to the way you wish it would be or some imaginary standard. This is not pasting positive thoughts over negative beliefs. Some examples of positive contexts could be:

• Extending unconditional love to all parts of yourself, especially to those feelings you haven't liked in the past

• Being grateful that the experience is not worse

• Enjoy being on the threshold of change

• Noticing that what you are experiencing is funny

• Being grateful you have all the emotional components of a fully functioning human being

An imaginary standard is something like: how it should be, how good it used to be, how you wish it were, or how somebody else has it. So at your present weight, perhaps you're making yourself wrong for not being thinner. Really, you could be grateful that you're as thin as you are, but if you are comparing yourself to an imaginary standard about how thin you should be, you're making yourself wrong and being negative towards yourself. When we feel negative toward ourselves, we often resist the feelings, and do anything we can to not feel that feeling, which starts a downward cycle of negativity from which we try to escape by eating.

When you use the Vivation process, you learn to acknowledge, accept and even to enjoy the feelings in your body that you have formerly tried to escape from or avoid. When you shift the way you feel about something or the way you think about it, that shift causes you to no longer resist the feelings in your body so you no longer have to suppress them with food or any other substance. This is what we call "integration," the ability to have all of your feelings and emotions contribute to your well-being.

Making lemonade from life's lemons

To understand this more, try to remember an experience you've had that you didn't enjoy at the time, but now you can look back on it and realize that it was a good thing. For example, many people have had the experience of breaking up with their first sweetheart. Most people start out thinking of this experience as uncomfortable and very negative, but as you can now look back and realize, ultimately it was for your benefit. If you can experience your gratitude for all the relationships you've had since then, you realize that you would not have been able to experience them if you hadn't broken up with your first lover, and you can experience gratitude for breaking up with that person. Learning to relate to an initially painful experience with gratitude changes the feelings in your body and allows you to feel good about yourself, and this is what we call integration.

Can you think of any other experience you've had that you didn't enjoy at the time but you can look back on it and know that it was all for the best? Developing your ability to integrate allows you to telescope, or reduce, the time between an experience and your recognition of it as being beneficial. If you can relate to the experience as beneficial, you can feel good about it. Even if it was a horrible experience, you can be grateful that you had the strength to survive it, and that in itself is a positive context. Holding something in a positive context is not positive thinking about a horrible circumstance, it allows you to heal the inner pain at a very deep level by appreciating your strengths more.

You choose your experience

To further illustrate the idea that you can choose to change the way you perceive something, here's an example: Do you know that how you think about a half-filled glass of water affects your happiness? Is the glass half-empty or half-full? If you perceive it as being half-empty, you can bemoan the fact that you don't have more water, wonder what you did to deserve so little water, etc., which causes you to have certain feelings in your body of limitation and suffering. On the other hand, you could choose to endlessly celebrate the half-full glass of water, be grateful about it, think about how lucky you are, celebrate water-drinkers everywhere. It's completely up to you. The glass of water does not change, but you are deeply affected by how you think about it. By choosing to look at the situation in a certain way, you create uncomfortable feelings in your body that you must deal with somehow. Compulsive eating is one of the least successful ways you can deal with those feelings. Any time you are unhappy with your present circumstances, it is because you are comparing the way it is to an imaginary standard of how you think it should be.

How to shift your experience to a positive context

In Loving Yourself Thin, you learn to be your own best friend and cheerleader. That means you lovingly accept yourself for the purposes of creating the ideal body that you want from a place of positivity. We have already noted that whenever you make yourself wrong, you have unpleasant feelings in your body that you must attempt to suppress by eating. This leads to a downward spiral of frustration, self-loathing, more eating, and so on. So it is very beneficial for you to develop a technique of making yourself right by learning to shift your relationship to the feelings in your body.

Vivation is a powerful process that includes circular breathing (connected breathing), focused awareness of the feelings and conscious relaxation. The entire process is best learned initially with a coach, in the setting of a private session or seminar. However, it is possible to create similar benefits by learning to shift context mentally, and you will be able to experience the changes in your feelings. Here's a process to help you learn how to integrate your negative feelings. Remember that this is a tool and that you have to really engage yourself and make an effort for it to work for you.

1. Make a list of ten things that you don't like about your body, your relationship to food, or anything at all. Notice that when you contemplate the ten things on your list, you get unpleasant feelings in your body that you would probably prefer not to feel, or at the very least, don't enjoy. Let yourself feel them and don't eat.

2. Begin to compare the things on your ten things list with the list below: "How to Shift Anything to a Positive Context." Start with the first thing on your list and compare it with the first thing on this list. Begin to think about the item on your list in the positive context of the idea on the Positive Context list, and see if thinking about it differently changes the way you feel about it. Either it will or it won't and you'll be able to feel it either way. If it changes, fine, there's one

more thing to be happy about and enjoy in your life, but if it doesn't, go on to the next thing on the Positive Context list and think about your item in relation to this. If it does integrate, then go on to both the next thing on your list and the next thing on the Positive Context list and do it again. If it does not integrate, stay on your same item and keep applying different positive context to it until it shifts in your mind. The way you will know that it integrates is by paying attention to your feelings. If you continue to have an unpleasant feeling, it means that you are still making it wrong. If you are able to shift the context and integrate the negativity, you will feel better when you think about it.

For the purpose of this process, you should consider it an integration if you feel your energy move in the direction of feeling good about something you formerly felt bad about. Your feelings about something can still be a little bit unresolved, and yet you can feel a whole lot better about it.

All you need to do is find three or four statements that work for you among all of the ones below, and you will be well on your way to making a quantum leap in enjoying more of your life.

How to Shift Anything to a Positive Context

1. Find a way to enjoy it.

2. Notice that what you are experiencing is not infinitely bad. Be grateful that it's as good
as it is.

3. Expand your gratitude for your existence to include the particulars of what you are experiencing now. Surrender to the fact that your life is the way it is whether you resist
it or not.

4. Just decide to accept it.

5. Cultivate a sense of fascination with it. Let it engage your natural feelings of curiosity.

6. Expand your compassion for all people who experience similar things.

7. Expand your compassion for yourself for having struggled with this for as long as you have.

8. Think about someone or a pet you love deeply and send that same love to the feeling
inside you.

9. Be open to this feeling making a contribution to you somehow.

10. Extend unconditional love to all parts of your experience, including what you're feeling right now.

11. Be grateful you are strong enough to have survived your past.

12. Enjoy the newness of the feeling; or, take comfort in the familiarity.

Points to remember

In addition to learning to shift the way you relate to the feelings, if is helpful to remember the following points while doing Vivation:

1. Notice where the feelings are in your body. Focus on and inhale through the strongest feeling. Feelings can be emotions, physical sensations or patterns of energy. Breathe comfortably in a way that the inhale is connected to the exhale, so there are no pauses in between. Relax on the exhale, rather than blowing it out.

2. Focus your awareness on the feelings closely enough so that you can feel when they change.

3. Enjoy the feelings as much as you can, and relax.

You can use the LYT companion Vivation CD set to begin to experience this powerful healing technique on your own. Go to www.vivationusa.com to purchase. In addition, Vivation is taught internationally by Vivation professionals in private sessions, group classes and seminars. Go to www.vivation.com to find out more.

For further reading about the Vivation process, read *The Skill of Happiness: Creating Daily Ecstasy with Vivation* by Jim Leonard (available at bookstores or www.vivation.com,) *Vivation: The Skill of Happiness* by Jim Leonard and Phil Laut, and *Your Fondest Dream: The Power of Creativity*, by Jim Leonard.

Homeplay

Every day this week, choose and use some Positive Context statement that will help you shift the context about whatever you're feeling and use that statement throughout the day.

To illustrate, if you have chosen the statement, "I'm open to this feeling contributing to me in some way," you could use that to gain insight about why you are having those feelings, and further, allow that curiosity to help you feel better about the feelings. For example, if you are a survivor of incest, you could quietly relax and begin to acknowledge the feeling of strength that you have as an inner resource that helped you get through it. Notice that this resource has helped you survive as well as you have, as things could always be worse. This could lead you to have compassion for those who experienced the same thing and therefore have more compassion for yourself. In this way, you consciously turn feelings which detract from your sense of well-being into feelings of enjoyment.

Another example:

Let's say you have about a zillion things on your "to-do" list, and you feel frantic about getting everything done. You could bounce off the walls or you could take five minutes, sit yourself down in a quiet place, connect your breath, relax your muscles and say to yourself, "In what way can I be grateful for this?" There are probably as many ways to feel good about what's going on as there are on the to-do list, such as being grateful you have something to do, that you're the kind of conscientious person who makes an effort to get their tasks done, that you are enthusiastic about getting them done completely and in record time. These thoughts will give you pleasure about yourself, instead of discomfort that more isn't getting done in the same time.

So every day this week, choose a different "integrative" idea; when you notice an uncomfortable feeling, connect your inhale to your exhale, relax, become more aware of the feelings in your body, say the Positive Context statement to yourself and see what happens. Be open to the feelings changing. If they don't, that's alright, acknowledge the feelings in a positive way, and let them be there. Just relaxing about the fact you are feeling them can change them, too. Most importantly, remember it's your willingness to improve the quality of your life that makes positive change happen.

All about exercise

Even though I don't tell people that they must exercise, I believe that being active should be included in any healthy lifestyle. But, if you've been forcing yourself to do something out of fear of gaining weight and not enjoying the activity, you're not going to keep it up anyway. You should do activities you enjoy, and if you get aerobic benefit, so much the better. Activities such as bowling, dancing or gardening are perfectly acceptable as exercise, too. Don't approach movement from the standpoint of how many calories you can burn doing this or that.

Just do what you enjoy and have fun. Concentrate at being proficient at it and mastering whatever it takes to improve.

Write out responses to the following statements.

Ideas I have about exercise...(Everyone looks at me and I feel criticized, etc.) _____

_____

Reasons I like to move...(I love rhythm and dancing, etc.) _____

_____

Why I dislike movement...(You get all sweaty, etc.) _____

_____

Excuses I have used for not exercising_____

_____

Some of the physical activities I'd enjoy doing if I were my ideal weight _____

_____

What keeps me from doing these things at my present weight _____

_____

2. Affirmations

After giving yourself literally millions of negative self-talk messages over the years, you need to not only become aware of these self-criticisms and their effect on you, but also to consciously change such comments, so that positive statements, rather than negative ones, become more automatic. Try saying the following affirmations aloud (while driving in the car, in the shower, whenever you are alone and have the opportunity, and silently to yourself at other times during the day.) Or try writing them down here and noting your response.

Choose any of these affirmations which appeal to you, or create your own. Use at least three over the next week.

I, _____, accept my body as it is; it has served me well. Now I am safely letting go of excess weight.

I, _____, love myself and my body unconditionally.

I, _____, am learning to feed myself with the things that satisfy me.

I, _____, can lose weight by loving myself completely.

The more I relax about my body and eating, the less important food is for me.

It is easy for me, _____, to love myself.

I, _____, am now eating my way to thinness.

I, _____, forgive myself for eating when I was not hungry.

I, _____, deserve to achieve and maintain my perfect weight, no matter what I eat.

I am getting better and better every day, because I love and appreciate myself more.

This Week:

Eat when you are hungry

Eat whatever you want to eat

Eat until you are satisfied

If you overeat this week, notice your thoughts and feelings about it and write them down here:

Why did you overeat? _____

What messages do you give yourself either while you're eating or after? _____
_____

What was going on for you before you overate? _____

Can you be gentle and forgiving with yourself?

Chapter Ten
Living for Today

Honoring Yourself with Food

Honoring yourself with food is about finding a way to eat that will increasingly contribute to your well-being, no matter what it is you are feeding yourself. There are no bad foods and you should never tell yourself that you are bad for eating anything.

Honoring yourself with food means that you are giving yourself what you want, and you not only find out exactly what you need to feel satisfied, but you think about how the food is going to affect you, physically and emotionally. This chapter is about taking responsibility for your food choices, and accepting those choices, whatever they may be. Based on your values of what you want for yourself, about which you are getting more and more clear, you decide if you want to eat a certain food. Ask yourself if the food honors the person you want to be, the person that you're becoming.

The point of all this is, of course, that you know that you can have it, but do you really want it? Do you want the momentary satisfaction of the food in your mouth and stomach, or do you want the deeper satisfaction of knowing that you're helping yourself achieve your ideal body? Either choice is okay, and you make it okay with yourself, knowing that when you're ready to make the changes, they will happen spontaneously, not by forced denial or restriction. When you remove all the shame and "shoulds", what's left is what's your choice in the matter. This is truly taking responsibility for yourself.

You're in the process of change, and you are in the process of becoming a different kind of person than you were before you had this much awareness of your food habits. Find out if you are using food to fix some kind of hunger other than physical hunger. If you are feeling hungry for something else, it's important to address that hunger directly, rather than use food to try to solve it.

You are becoming the kind of person that deals with their desires directly rather than suppressing emotions and using food or your body shape as a distraction. Will eating get you what you really want, like a hug or some loving attention? If it won't, you may want to think twice about your actions. If food won't solve your issue in the moment, then why eat? For example, if you're angry with your mate, you sometimes get the urge to eat chocolate. But you recognize the feeling for what it is: a desire to suppress your feelings of anger and lose yourself for the moment in sensory pleasure. But you will also come to know that indeed, the chocolate itself won't do anything about your angry feelings, and in fact, if you binge on chocolate at that point, you'll be even more upset. So you can look past the desire of the immediate moment to see that eating will not solve your problem of being upset with your mate. You need to do something directly with that situation and not try to use food to make it go away or to distract yourself.

As you begin to realize that food won't solve your problems, you can be more selective about when and how much you eat. It is important to understand that this is a trial and error process, and don't expect yourself to be excellent at it right away. You might eat something out of habit, but after doing that a certain number of times and noticing that it doesn't work for you, you may decide not to continue eating like that. It is also important to be gentle with yourself no matter what you're doing, understanding that by allowing yourself to have what you want, you will naturally grow out of eating for non-hunger reasons, when food stops serving a purpose for you other than satisfying hunger.

The basis for change: accepting yourself as you are right now

Decide that you will accept yourself as you are now and that you are in the process of change, no matter what anyone else says about what you are doing. If you encounter people in your life who want to judge and evaluate you, thank them for sharing, but don't let their feelings or opinions sabotage you in making the decision to love and accept yourself. You know what you are trying to accomplish, and what you are doing with this program.

What this comes down to is learning about your own values and realities, how you are going to view your body, your relationship to food and what you want in life. Don't let external factors and the people around you change your feelings about what's right for you. The more you are empowered with feeling good about yourself, the stronger you become about asserting yourself regarding what you need and want and what you don't want in your life.

When you accept and honor yourself as you are now, the better you feel about yourself and the easier it is to change. This doesn't mean that you lie to yourself and refuse to acknowledge any negativity, but let yourself be where you are gracefully, accepting that you're working on yourself, doing the best you can and that willingness is enough to create the change you're seeking.

People love to give unsolicited advice about how you should be. But have courage and listen to your own counsel. Discard old or erroneous ideas about how you should live your life if these old ideas don't fit in with your new process of treating yourself with love, respect and acceptance of everything about yourself, including your body and your relationship with food.

As you shift your inner perception about yourself, regardless of your outer physical appearance, other people's perception of you will shift. Work with your thoughts and feelings, and as you start to feel better about yourself, you will radiate a different energy. You will look different. You will start to relate to yourself differently. Work on integrating your suppressed emotions using Vivation, and you can change dramatically.

Living in the Present

Do you have a number of different wardrobes to match your different size selves?

Do you have a range of sizes in your closet, from the super "skinny" clothes, to the really "fat" clothes? Are you holding on to clothes that may have fit you long ago, but don't anymore? You may have these things from when you were younger and smaller that you just can't bear to get rid of. But every time you look at them, you feel bad, because not only do they serve as a silent reminder that you've gained weight, but you feel that it would be a waste of money to throw them out. Perhaps it's time to go through your closet and get rid of some of the items that perhaps fit you years ago and that you've been saving for the time you can fit back into them. Go through and give away, or at least pack up and put in a box somewhere out of sight, the clothes that aren't in alignment with where your body is right now. If once a day you go to your closet and you've got mostly clothes that don't fit or look good on you right now, it's making you feel bad because you can't wear them anymore. You don't need that.

Swap or sweep

So have a garage sale, or a clothing swap with friends, or donate them to charity. You don't need these silent witnesses in your closet staring at you everyday, making you feel bad about the size you are now. Get them out of your life. Treat yourself, and buy a couple of new items that really fit you well, and look great on you. Take the time and along with a good, honest friend, periodically purchase something that makes the most of your good features: a nice bust, long legs, a small waist, or your pretty neck or face. Make sure that you know that when you put this outfit on, you'll feel like absolute dynamite, because this is an outfit that really expresses you, not your body size.

Loving Yourself Thin is about honoring yourself, and accepting yourself where you are now, feeling good in your clothes and what you're wearing, no matter what your size. Get clothes that fit, that aren't too tight, that don't feel uncomfortable, that feel wonderful to wear. Cleaning out your closet and living in the present gives you a lot of extra closet space, and allows you to recognize that, "OK, this is where I am now, this is my starting point, this is the first day of the rest of my life," and move on from there. Doesn't it make sense that if your body size does happen to get smaller, wouldn't you much rather go shopping and get some new things than wear your old clothes that might be out of style?

Are you postponing life until you are the right size?

As we talked about briefly in chapter seven, "Taking your life off hold...," there is nothing except your own beliefs and emotions that are keeping you from following your dreams and doing what you want regardless of your size.

Make the decision that you will not allow your size to keep you from going after what you want in life. Look for role models in whatever it is that you have the desire to do. You will find that there are role models of all sizes doing absolutely everything! Look around and you'll see. There are large size fashion models, comics, ice skaters, dancers, fashion consultants. Your thoughts about it and the way you are relating to the activity are really the only things that are keeping you from doing it.

Start right now and make a list of some of the things you might really like to do in your life, and consider what kind of thoughts you have about actually getting out there and doing them. Write down some of your favorite excuses, and the most logical reasons for NOT doing the things you want to do. Then ask yourself if you are willing to postpone your happiness until some day that might never arrive. As you come to see that it is only your thoughts and beliefs about them that is keeping you from living the fuller, more satisfying life you want, see if you'd be willing to begin to live your life on a grander scale by including those things that you will find satisfying and fulfilling.

Chapter Eleven
Put it all Together for the Life You Want

In the preceding pages, you have been presented with some very powerful ideas about how to reach and maintain your ideal weight by not using food for anything other than fueling your body. You also have some good ideas about how to go after and get the things that you want in your life by raising your self-esteem, and believing that you deserve to have what you want, no matter what your size. You've learned some very powerful ways of nurturing yourself, how to be more gentle with yourself and how to be your own best friend.

As you practice and go through the homeplay and exercises, you will start to examine many of the real issues that cause you to keep on extra weight There are many levels for which you to examine these issues, and its all part of an ongoing learning process about you, about what makes you tick and why you are the way you are. Everything that you discover about yourself in this process is valuable and has the potential to assist you in becoming happier and more fulfilled in your life. When you recognize there is something making you unhappy, you have the option of changing it, accepting it or both. Either way, you have become aware of a method of resolving something that has been causing you discomfort, and if you can see it clearly, you are more in a position to do something about it.

Recognize that your excess weight and body have served you in a lot of positive ways. Perhaps it's protected you and allowed you to feel strong and powerful, or it's been a message to the people against whom you've wanted to rebel. Look at the ways that maybe weight has served you and see if you can't come up with some other ways of creating the same outcome. Perhaps it would be learning to be more assertive with people, so that you don't need to carry the extra weight to protect yourself from unkind remarks from family members or the outside world.

Perhaps you've been using your weight as an issue to distract yourself from other problems in your life that seem unsolvable. If weight were not an issue for you, you would have to address those other problems, so why not start thinking about how loving and valuing yourself could help you to find creative ways to tackle those problems?

You will be living with your body for your entire life. Wouldn't you rather be friends than constantly battling yourself? By dieting, you could reach your ideal weight and stay there for a while, but it is not a long term solution. Now that you are aware that food is not really the problem, you know that it is the underlying feelings and emotions that need to be addressed, and you have some tools with which to do that.

So this is a lifelong process about becoming happier and more comfortable with the unique and perfect individual that you are. As you put these guidelines to work and lose some weight, you must be on guard about slipping back into the diet mentality. You might lose a few pounds, your body changes and you feel really good about yourself. Then you start to calculate, "Gee, if I keep going at this rate, I'll be such and such a weight at such and such a time, and I can do this or that, and wear that dress..." Well, that's the diet mentality reaching out to grab you all over again! That's thinking again that fat is bad and thin is good, and that you can't be okay the way you are now. You might lose some weight, and then as you get to more subtle levels of your issues about food and your weight, you stop and are at a plateau for a while. Your mind will probably play games to trick you into the diet mentality again, because if you don't continue to lose weight at the same pace, you will make yourself wrong and feel bad and the entire downward spiral starts again.

As you start to feel better about yourself and your body as it is now, don't lose sight of the strength of the diet mentality conditioning and messages from our society that have had a hold on you for a long, long time. When this comes up, stop and tell yourself that you're okay as you are, you're taking care of yourself with this process and that it will continue to work for you. You're really healing yourself on a permanent level. Make it okay that you won't diet to fit into that dress or ever fast again because you don't like the way you look in the mirror. Such deprivation and self-negation is simply not a part of your life anymore. It's going to take time, and because the way you are right now is okay, you might as well start loving yourself just as you are. There is nothing sadder that the thought that you postpone living and loving because of an extra ten pounds that you think make you look ugly.

Handling your compulsive overeating doesn't mean you are automatically expected to handle everything else in your life. You will constantly face new challenges in life and find that the grass isn't necessarily greener as a thin person. You will still have issues in your life to handle, but with these tools and principles, you will have what you need to believe in yourself, and have the self-esteem to tackle and solve your problems without using food. You will be able to be on your own side, ask for the help you need and bring yourself up whenever you need a boost.

I am here to help you achieve your goals - write to me at pb@vivationusa.com with any questions or comments regarding Loving Yourself Thin or Vivation. Our website address is www.vivationusa.com.

Good luck with the guidelines and principles I've given you. There is a lot here to assimilate and put into practice, but you can take it a step at a time, being gentle and loving with yourself. Remember that you can't nag or beat yourself into self-improvement, so the best strategy is always to love yourself and make changes from that positive point.

www.ingramcontent.com/pod-product-compliance
Lightning Source LLC
Chambersburg PA
CBHW081459040426
42446CB00016B/3307